From Sigriswil to Nappanee: 300 Years of Stähli History

REVISED AND UPDATED

From Sigriswil to Nappanee: 300 Years of Stähli History

REVISED AND UPDATED

Bruce W. Stahly

Cover:
Sigriswil und Thunersee, von Nordosten.
⊜ Jakob Samuel Weibel (1771–1846),
Swiss National Library.

Opposite Title Page:
Alpine vista, from the north shore of Lake Thun.
Credit: Tom van Cleve

Back Cover:
Fanciful rendering of a farm (circa 1874) in Locke
Township, Elkhart County, Indiana.

The past is never dead. It's not even past.

—William Faulkner, **Requiem for a Nun**

Contents

Family Charts

Mainline

Spur

Author's Note

Researching a family history is a dynamic process: it is never complete, it is never perfect. New material appears, old assumptions are discarded, and errors are discovered. Since this book was originally published in 2016, new details have emerged about the families presented here. Some of those details have now been incorporated into this revised edition, although the scope of the overall book remains unchanged. The "Sources" section has been replaced by a bibliography, and I have made other format changes. Errors which have been identified by attentive readers, or that I have discovered myself, have been corrected.

Bruce W. Stahly
March 2024

Introduction

This family history traces my Stähli paternal heritage from mid 17th century Switzerland to the 20th century in Indiana.

Writing a family history presents many challenges. There is the research and verification of data from hundreds of years in the past, with the usual problems of access, language, difficult handwriting, and ambiguous and/or contradictory information.

Another problem, which has overwhelmed many family historians, is the exponential nature of genealogical research. The number of every person's ancestors doubles in each generation: all individuals have two parents, four grandparents, eight great-grandparents, etc.

Working six or eight generations in the past, a diligent researcher could be dealing with between 256 to 1024 grandparents.[1] Obviously, it is impossible to trace and document all of these separate lines of ancestry, and still maintain some sort of outside life. So choices have to be made.

The scope of this history is limited to my own paternal ancestry, which can first be documented in the 17th century in Switzerland. I have chosen to end this particular history with my paternal grandfather, Roy Stahly, who was born in 1893 and died in 1986. There are many descendants of Roy Stahly and his wife, Ethel Frederick, who share this ancestry. Their details are not included in this book. It is for these descendants that this book is intended.

Why have I chosen this approach? It is personal: this history documents my own paternal heritage, and this heritage, as is usual (though by no means universal) in Western societies, follows the surname, which is the surname that I bear.

This is a minuscule fragment of my ancestry, and it is neither more nor less important than all the other fragments. However, it is the one that I am following in this history, for better or worse.

The easiest way to document one's genealogical past is through the use of software. Much of the genealogical history in this book is based on a database that has been compiled over many years. It is difficult—maybe impossible—to make the contents of a family tree database very interesting in book form. Long lists of

---

1   Although they may not be **unique** individuals, since cousins marrying each other would reduce the number of unique grandparents.

ancestors and descendants are not very enjoyable to read.

In this book, I have used genealogical charts to accompany the text. Hopefully, this makes the information easier to understand. The main genealogical line that is covered in this history is illustrated on the first chart, called Mainline 1, on page 14. Using a train metaphor, this is the "mainline" of research, with some spur or branch lines leading off of it.

Each "station" (i.e., individual) on this "mainline" chart points to the same individual on a subsequent chart, where that person's details are expanded.

There are other charts—"spurs"—i.e., branches, which document a collateral genealogy, such as the ancestors of a spouse, or the descendants of a sibling of a person on the "mainline." These are "spur lines" only in the context of this book.[2]

This simplified approach means that many details have been omitted. Siblings, spouses, children, and collateral lines are not shown except in selected cases.

This book has been organized into chapters (1–4) that follow the geographic locations (Switzerland, Germany, the United States) of the family. It starts in the town of Sigriswil, on the north shore of Lake Thun, in Canton Bern, Switzerland, and ends in Indiana, in the United States, about 300 years later. Of course, Switzerland is not really the beginning and Indiana is not really the end. But that is the scope of this history.

---

2   Full exploration of the thousands of people who descend from these lines is outside the scope of this book.

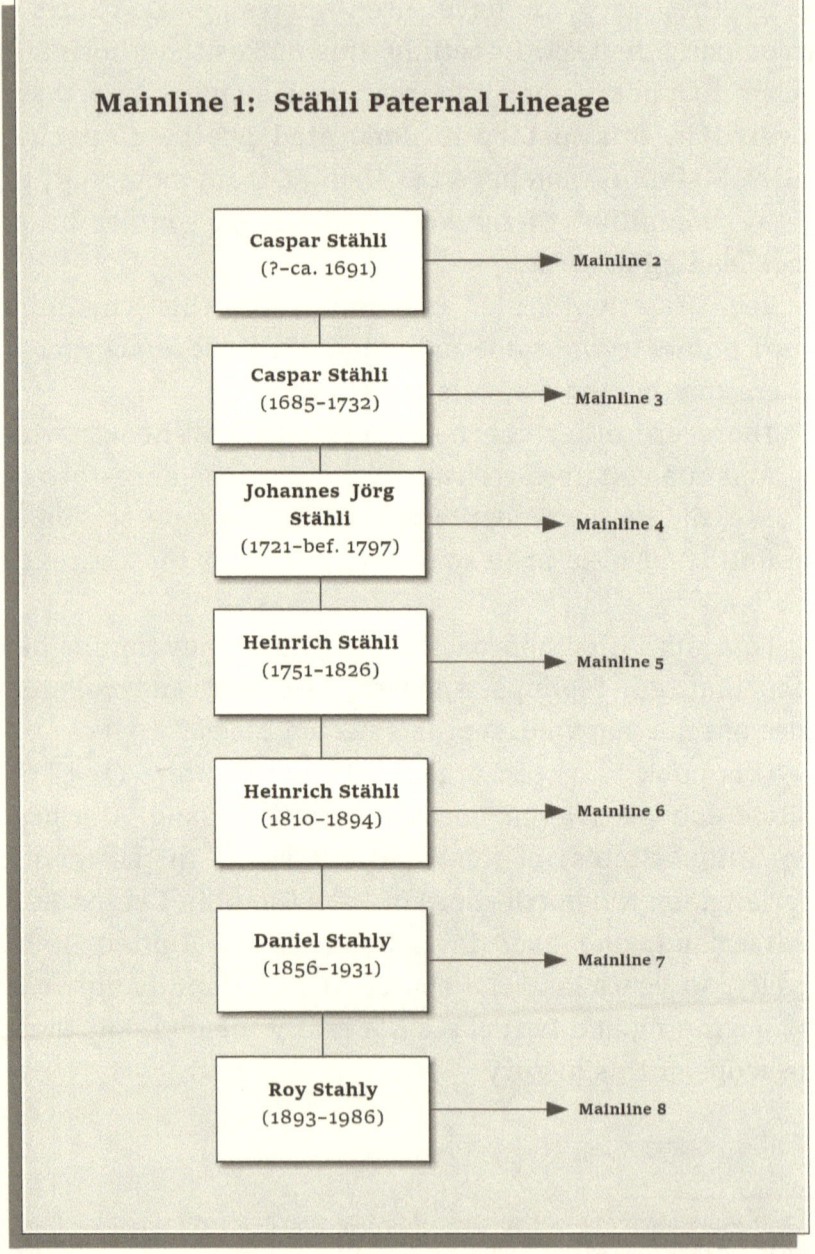

Mainline 1: Stähli Paternal Lineage

Caspar Stähli
(?–ca. 1691) → Mainline 2

Caspar Stähli
(1685–1732) → Mainline 3

Johannes Jörg Stähli
(1721–bef. 1797) → Mainline 4

Heinrich Stähli
(1751–1826) → Mainline 5

Heinrich Stähli
(1810–1894) → Mainline 6

Daniel Stahly
(1856–1931) → Mainline 7

Roy Stahly
(1893–1986) → Mainline 8

Chapter 5 is a brief look at some interesting genealogies that intersect with that of the Stähli family.

Chapter 6 summarizes the story of the story, i.e., the process of collecting the data and stories that make up this family history.

Family researchers typically work backward in time, out of necessity, researching each previous generation as names and dates are discovered. Since the main thread of this book moves forward in time, I decided to confine the meta-story to a separate chapter.

The Afterword provides some details on how family members can use the data in this book to extend their own family history, using their own data and stories.

Surnames have been standardized to the modern forms used today in Switzerland, Germany and North America. I have also used modern spellings for place names. Many of the place names mentioned in this book still exist: they can be located using Google Maps, or similar software. Two maps are included in this book for easy reference.

Stähli Name

The Stähli surname has undergone various changes in the years since the family left Switzerland for the German Palatinate (or the Pfalz, as it will be known in this book), and subsequently emigrated to the United States. In very early entries in the Hilterfingen and Sigriswil parish registers, the name was spelled 'Stäli.' Only later was the 'h' used in the entries.

The name appears in several locations throughout Switzerland and persists to the present day.

There were/are Stähli families in Oberhofen am Thunersee, Hilterfingen, Brienz, Burgdorf, Bern, Meiringen, Interlaken, and other places in Canton Bern and across Switzerland. These appear to be unrelated families, without genetic connections.

The surname is probably occupational, i.e., derived from a craft. *Stahl* is the German word for "steel," so it is likely that somewhere in early days, a family progenitor was a craftsman in hardened metals.

Since many towns and villages needed such a craftsman, it is not surprising that numerous, independent, unrelated families would come to bear the name. The 'i' suffix makes the name distinctly Swiss, and is the result of the Swiss penchant for diminutives. Essentially, "Stähli" is the Swiss equivalent of the German "Schmidt" or the English "Smith."

In Germany, the name became "Staehly." An 'a' with an umlaut (ä) is the equivalent of 'ae', so the only change the Germans made was to substitute a 'y' for the 'i'. English speakers also adopted the 'y' substitution, but most also dropped the umlaut or its equivalent 'ae', retaining only the 'a'—though some families in the United States did retain the 'ae'. And, of course, there are many alternative spellings.

"Stähli" seems to be a distinctly Bernese spelling of the name. One family in Canton Zürich spelled their name "Stehli," which in turn became "Stehly" in North America.

For this book, I use the modern Swiss spelling of the family name for those individuals who were born and lived in Europe. Emigrants to North America, of course, probably used one version of their surname in Europe and an anglicized version after they crossed the ocean.

An individual may appear, in this book, under slightly different names. For married women, I employ her birth surname, rather than a husband's surname.

Records

The Swiss data from early times in this history has been extracted from Swiss parish registers, which are handwritten records of births, marriages and deaths compiled (in Canton Bern) from the time of the Reformation.

Canton Bern has preserved these valuable resources in the cantonal archives in the city of Bern. Most can be accessed in digital form on the web site of the Canton Bern archives. (The full web address is specified in the Bibliography, page 185.) In the archives are digital copies of the parish registers of 177 parishes within the canton. Each parish's records may contain hundreds of handwritten pages. The records have not been transcribed, and there is no search function.

There are the usual challenges in the handwriting, ambiguity of language, and the problems created when multiple individuals in a locality share the same first name and surname.

Baptisms, as recorded in the local parish register, typically occurred within a week or two of a child's birth. The actual date of birth was not usually recorded, especially in very early records. The birth years given here, for individuals born in Switzerland, may actually be the baptism year. Of course, the birth year and baptism year were almost always the same, except when a child was born in the last week or two in December.

Records from Germany are not as thorough. The fragmented political structure of the Pfalz meant that record-keeping was often inconsistent from place to place. In addition, the Amish-Mennonite community (which is crucial to this history) was always very small relative to the larger population, and their non-conformist, insular instincts meant that they were often outside mainstream religious, social and political institutions. Archion, a German subscription-based service, has digitized many parish registers in Germany.

In the United States, the Federal Census conducted every ten years is a very valuable resource, especially starting in 1850, when all individuals in a household were explicitly identified. By using the place of birth usually included with an individual's entry in the census, much can be deduced about family migrations.

Terminology

I use the term "Anabaptist" to refer to the non-conforming sect of Christianity that had its beginnings in Europe in the 16th century. "Anabaptist" is an umbrella term that includes the Amish and the Mennonites, as well as other groups which are not involved in this history. Later, as my story moves out of Switzerland, I use the terms "Amish," "Mennonite," or "Amish-Mennonite." I employ these terms more or less interchangeably, without concern for the doctrinal differences that separate the various groups, either in the past or today. Only when I use the term "Old Order Amish" do I specifically mean those conservative groups who maintain the conspicuously traditional life style thought of today as "Amish."

1. Along the *Thunersee*

Early Traces

The oldest remaining trace of this Stähli family in the Sigriswil area is from 1653, in the parish church of Hilterfingen, situated on the north shore of the *Thunersee* (Lake Thun), Canton Bern, Switzerland. There, Battin Saurer and Christina von Gunten baptized a son with the given name Christian. One of the witnesses was Caspar Stähli, of Aeschlen. This man could be the Caspar Stähli (died before 1673) on Mainline Chart 2 (page 28).

Ten years later, in 1663, Caspar Stähli was a witness at the baptism of Ulrich Amstutz, the son of Hans Amstutz and his wife Barbara Boss. This family lived in Aeschlen; therefore, the baptism took place in the old Sigriswil church, which burned a few years later.

A sales contract from 1668 refers to a piece of land that was adjacent to the vineyard of Caspar Stähli,[1] of Aeschlen. Five years later, in 1673, another sales contract relating to a piece of land in Aeschlen described the parcel as being adjacent to that of the "late Caspar Stähli." As the Caspar Stähli (died ca. 1691) was still alive in 1673, this reference could refer to his father, the oldest Caspar Stähli (died before 1673), who was likely the man named as a witness at the baptisms in 1653 and 1663. The surname "Saurer" belonging to the wife of Caspar Stähli (d. ca. 1691), as well as being the family name of the child at the 1653 baptism is also, perhaps, significant.

It is known from later baptismal records and sales contracts that Caspar Stähli (d. ca. 1691) was from Aeschlen. It is probable that all of these early references to Caspar Stähli of Aeschlen are about the same family, but it cannot be conclusively proven.

Before the birth of the son, Caspar (1673), it is clear that there were two men with that name, both of Aeschlen, and thus, most likely, father and son.

Aeschlen (officially, "Aeschlen ob Gunten") is a hamlet approximately 8 kilometers from the nearest city, Thun. It belongs to the community (*Gemeinde*) of Sigriswil. It was,

---

1   Altogether there were four males named Caspar Stähli. To differentiate them in the text, I have parenthetically appended baptism or death years after the name. Since the first three men named Caspar Stähli pass out of this history fairly quickly, I then use "Caspar Stähli" (without dates) to mean Caspar Stähli (1685-1732).

and remains, a small collection of houses on the steep hillside high above the *Thunersee*. A deep ravine separates the villages of Sigriswil and Aeschlen.

Sigriswil

Sigriswil is a *Gemeinde*, i.e., a civil municipality, consisting of eleven villages, all located on the north shore of the *Thunersee*. The nearest American equivalent to a *Gemeinde* is a county.

Germanic tribes, who had arrived from the north, settled the area along the north shore of the *Thunersee* thousands of years ago. These settlers likely populated the area along the lake shore at first, and later moved up the very steep slopes, which were used for vineyards and pasture land.

Two of *Gemeinde* Sigriswil's eleven villages, Gunten and Merligen, are located directly on the shore of the lake. The other nine, including Aeschlen, Sigriswil town, and Ringoldswil, are at an elevation 800 feet higher than the lake. Some of the highest peaks in the Swiss Alps are visible in the distance across the lake, which is glacier-blue, cold, and very beautiful. The pyramidal shape of the Niesen mountain dominates the south-facing view from Sigriswil and Aeschlen. East of the *Thunersee* is the *Brienzersee*, Lake Brienz, with Interlaken on the narrow isthmus in between. See the map on page 25.

In 1347, the inhabitants of Sigriswil purchased their independence from an impecunious Kyburg aristocrat. The community was incorporated into the Swiss canton of Bern, but has remained self-governing. Swiss-German is the primary language spoken in this area.

The parish (*Kirchgemeinde*) of Sigriswil was contiguous with its civil boundaries, except for the hamlet of Ringoldswil, which belonged to the parish of Hilterfingen.

The early church in this area was associated with the Roman Catholic abbey at Interlaken, which had patronage rights over certain vineyards and Alpine pastures in the area.

After the Reformation, Canton Bern established the Reformed Church, which became the official, state-sanctioned institution. In this way, the parish of Sigriswil became Reformed (Protestant).

By edict of the Bernese cantonal government, local parishes were required to maintain official registers of baptisms and marriages. A requirement for death registers was added later.

Sigriswil and Aeschlen

From about 1520 onward, all Bernese parishes created handwritten records containing this vital information. Civil registration began in Canton Bern in about 1875.

A church has stood on the high ground in the village of Sigriswil for hundreds of years. The current church was built in 1678/1679 after a fire damaged its predecessor and the parish house in 1671. As a result of that fire, the parish records from before 1671 were destroyed.

One of the items saved from the 1671 fire was the baptismal font (*"Taufstein"*) from 1506. The font bears the coats of arms of the donors, one of whom was Christian Stähli, a resident in the abbey at Interlaken. I do not know whether he had any connection with the Stähli family that lived at Aeschlen, but I like to imagine that generations of Stählis were baptized at this font.

Sigriswil Church and Parish House,© Jakob Samuel Weibel (1771–1846). (Swiss National Library)

The geography of Sigriswil and its surroundings makes farming difficult. Flat land is rare, and, where it occurs, it is in small parcels. The steep, south-facing slopes would suggest viticulture, and indeed this was one of main uses of the land until the beginning of the 20th century, at which point disease and competition ended large-scale cultivation of grapes in the area.

Dairy farming, which the Swiss have perfected, has always been important, and remains so today. Typically, cows are pastured during the summer months in the Alpine meadows, often in communal fields. Milk is made into cheese and stored in huts until the autumn, when the cows are brought back down to the village, where they remain until the spring brings fresh grasses to the pastures.

Baptismal Font (1506), Sigriswil Church

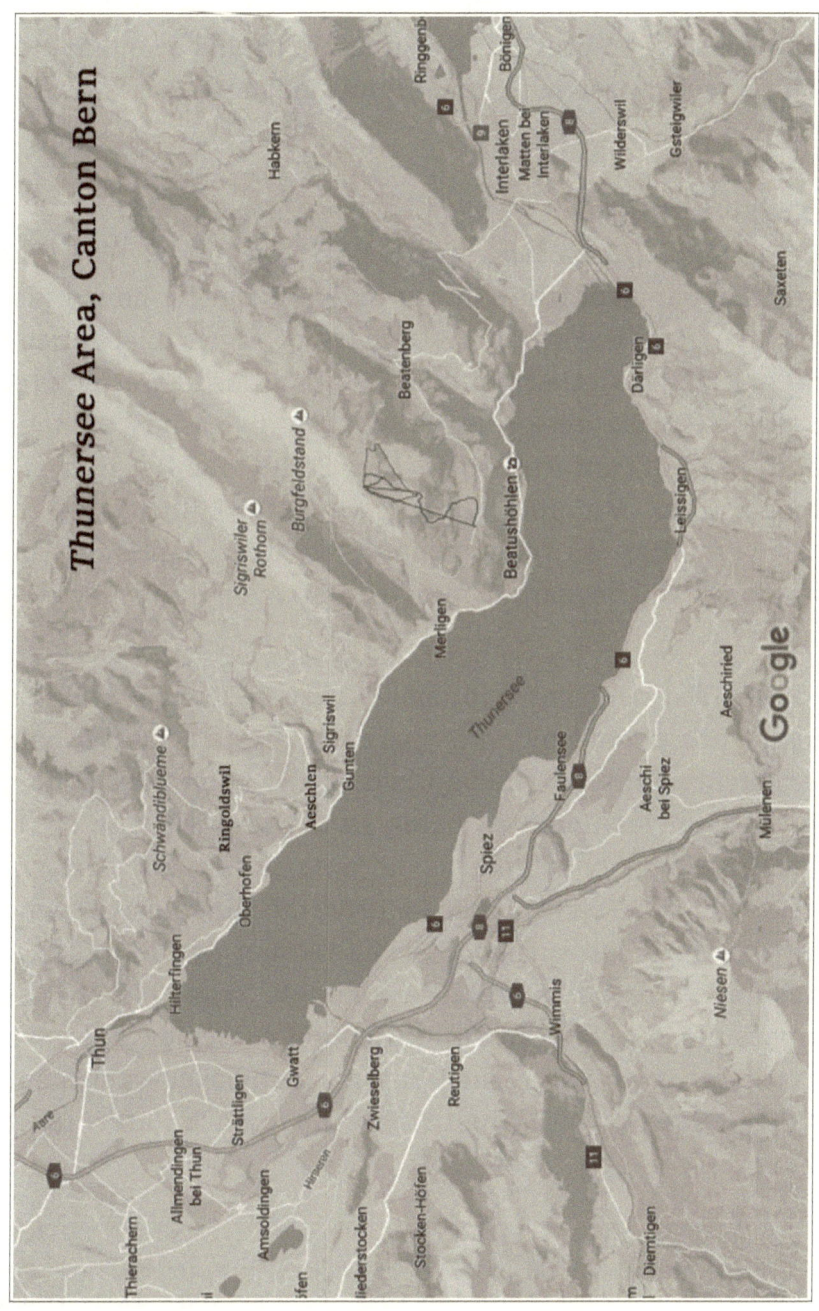

Thunersee Area, Canton Bern

Strict regulations limit the number of cows allowed to use a pasture, to prevent overgrazing. In this economy, the right to graze a cow in an Alpine meadow is a valuable commodity.

Sigriswil Stählis

The Sigriswil parish records begin on July 2, 1671. The fire that damaged the church and the parish house also destroyed the records of 150 years of Sigriswil baptisms and marriages to that point. A few families had attempted to re-construct the records of the baptisms of their children, but unfortunately the Stähli family was not among them. Mainline Chart 2 (page 28) illustrates the Stähli family, as documented by the baptisms and marriages in the parish register between the years 1673 and 1713.

The first relevant baptism is that of Caspar Stähli in 1673, presented by his parents Caspar Stähli and Benedichta Saurer.[2] The baptism occurred on July 6, 1673. The father was noted as being from Aeschlen, one of the eleven villages belonging to the municipality of Sigriswil. Baptismal witness Michael Saurer, of Ringoldswil, who, bearing the same surname as the mother of the infant, is presumed to be a relative—though what sort it is impossible to verify. In an interesting coincidence, he was married to a woman named Verena Schmocker—a surname that intersects with this Stähli line much later in its history.

---

2 Swiss parish registers usually record the mother's birth surname, rather than her husband's surname. Surnames of female baptismal witnesses are handled in the same way. This convention is extremely useful.

In Mainline Chart 2 (page 28), the grandfather of the child, Caspar (1673), is shown as Caspar Stähli (died before 1673). Although this is a reasonable assumption, it is unproven.

The Sigriswil parish register does not contain the marriage record of Caspar Stähli (d. ca. 1691) and Benedichta Saurer. Most likely the couple married before 1671, and thus the record was lost to the fire.

The chart also shows the existence of an older child, Hans, born sometime before the 1671 fire. The parish register does not record his baptism—his existence was not revealed until another document was discovered much later.

The Stähli-Saurer couple baptized their next child, Ulrich, in 1677. One of the witnesses at this baptism was Uli Saurer, brother of Michael Saurer, who had served as witness at the baptism of Caspar (1673). Little is known about Ulrich Stähli, except that a note in the margin next to his baptismal record indicates that he was issued a citizenship certificate for the Pfalz in 1701.

Apparently, Ulrich emigrated at about that time, but his further history is unknown. The Pfalz (or Palatinate) is an area in southwestern Germany, between the Rhine River in the east and France in the west.

A daughter, Anna, was baptized in 1680. Again, the baptismal record denotes Caspar Stähli (d. ca. 1691) as being from Aeschlen. In 1703, Anna Stähli married one of her neighbors, Jacob Racheter, as noted in the marriage register. By this time, the scribe had begun to write the surname with an 'h,' whereas in the earlier entries the surname had been written "Stäli."

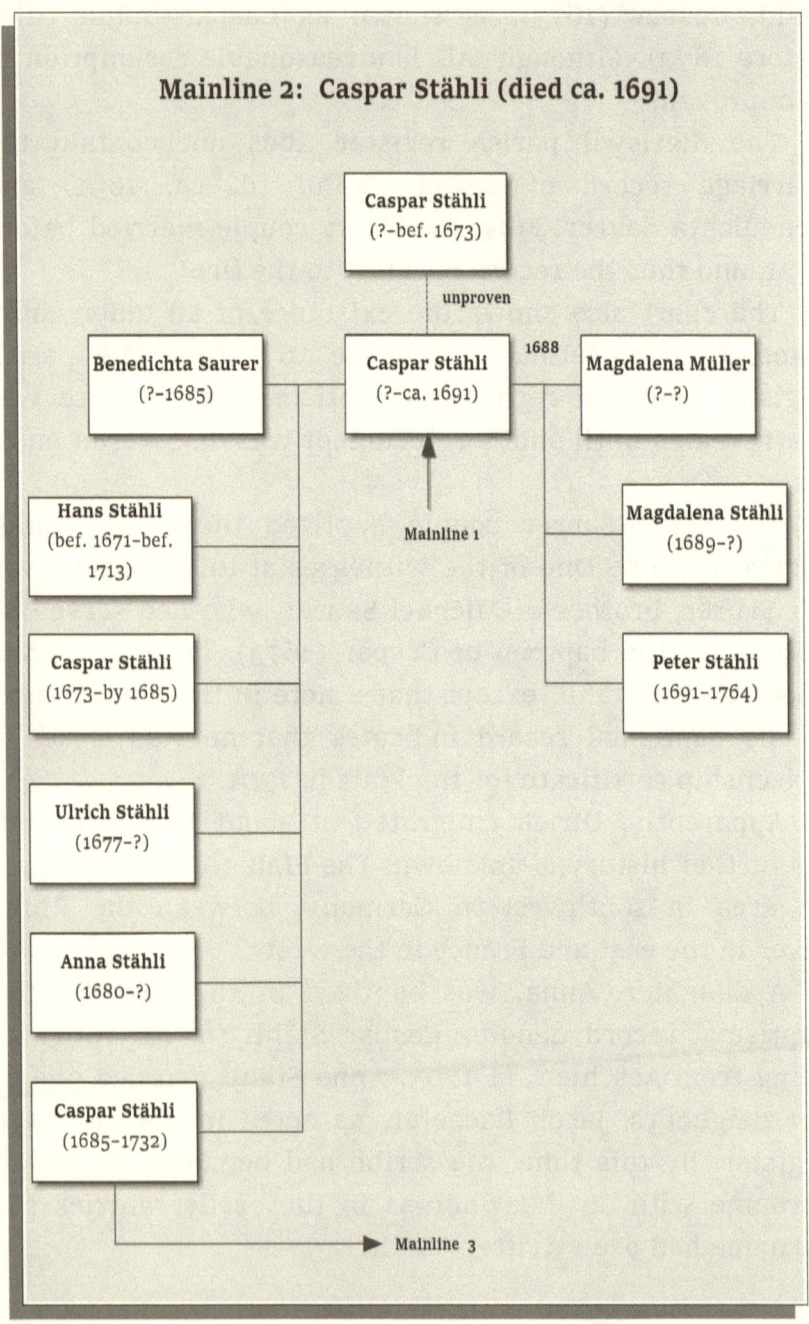

Mainline 2: Caspar Stähli (died ca. 1691)

Caspar Stähli
(?–bef. 1673)

unproven

Benedichta Saurer
(?–1685)

Caspar Stähli
(?–ca. 1691)

1688

Magdalena Müller
(?–?)

Mainline 1

Hans Stähli
(bef. 1671–bef. 1713)

Caspar Stähli
(1673–by 1685)

Ulrich Stähli
(1677–?)

Anna Stähli
(1680–?)

Caspar Stähli
(1685–1732)

Magdalena Stähli
(1689–?)

Peter Stähli
(1691–1764)

Mainline 3

Caspar Stähli (d. ca. 1691) and Benedichta Saurer baptized their last child, Caspar, on March 22, 1685. Since they christened him with same name as his older brother (born 1673), it is clear that the elder brother had died. At that time, it was not unusual for parents to christen a newborn child with the same name as a deceased elder sibling.

As Caspar Stähli (1685) is one of the main subjects of this history, it is worthwhile to include an image of his baptismal record from the Sigriswil parish register.

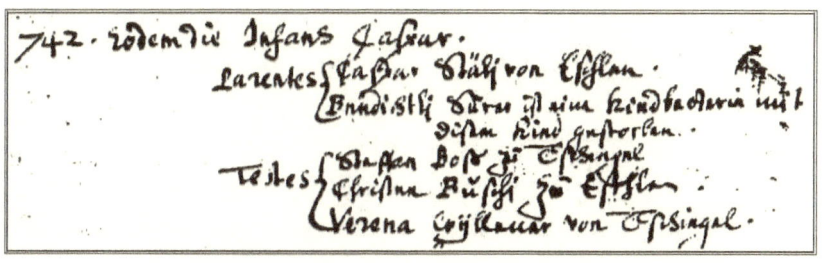

Caspar Stähli, baptism, Sigriswil Parish Register, 1685.

The transcription is:

742. *eodem die Infans Caspar*
       Parentes Caspar Stäli von Eschlen
         Benedichtli Surer ist eine Kindbetterin
         mit diesem Kind gestorben.
    Testes Steffan Boss zu Tschingel
        Christen Büschi zu Eschlen
        Verena Wyllener von Tschingel

This baptismal entry follows the typical form of Swiss records at that time. The baptismal date is given, followed by the infant's name, the names of the father and mother, and the names of the witnesses. This record is in a combination of Latin and German.

Freely translating this entry into English and standardizing surnames and place names, the result is:

> 742. *On the day noted above, infant Caspar*
> *Parents, Caspar Stähli of Aeschlen*
> *Benedichta Saurer, she died in*
> *childbirth with this child.*
> *Witnesses, Steffan Boss residing at Tschingel*
> *Christian Büschi residing at Aeschlen*
> *Verena Willener of Tschingel*

Since baptisms usually occurred on a Sunday, different families could present their children for baptism at the same time. In such cases, the parson (or scribe) would explicitly date the first entry. All subsequent baptisms on the same day would refer back to that date. In this case, the Latin phrase '*eodem die*' means 'on the same day.' Baptism sequence number 741, directly above this one in the parish register, was the first and only other baptism on that day, and was dated March 22 [1685].

The unusual Swiss system of citizenship is based on a municipality or locality. It is not dependent on place of birth (at the local level), but rather on the place (*Heimat*) where a family has historical right of citizenship. An individual could have citizenship rights in a far-distant Swiss village, but he or she might never have been there. These distinctions are present in the baptismal entry for Caspar Stähli, born 1685.

Where the baptismal entry denotes an individual with the German word *von*, he or she has citizenship rights in the locality named. An Individual denoted with the German word *zu* was residing in the locality named, but his or her citizenship rights were elsewhere. In English, *von* is translated as *from; zu* is translated as *at.* In this case, there are two witnesses who are designated as residing at Aeschlen or Tschingel. (Tschingel is one of the eleven villages of *Gemeinde* Sigriswil, and is adjacent to Aeschlen.)

Such distinctions were useful in identifying the person actually intended. A small, relatively closed, community limits the pool of available surnames and first names—there were often several people with identical first and last names. By adding a place of citizenship or residence after a person's name, the official records could differentiate individuals with the same name.

The crucial issue that arose when this 1685 baptismal entry was discovered focused on whether the child Caspar had survived. Although records found in Germany pointed back to this entry in the Sigriswil parish register, the language in the baptismal entry was ambiguous on whether the infant Caspar had survived into adulthood. It is clear, of course, that the mother had died in childbirth. But what about the child?

It was not unusual for stillborn infants to be given an emergency baptism. Infants who lived a few hours or days were also baptized. In such cases, in the Sigriswil parish register at that time, the parson added the word *"obit"* after the deceased infant's name. Latin for "he/she died," this notation appears frequently in the parish register, as the infant mortality rate was quite high.

In this case, as can be seen from the image of the baptismal record, no such notation was made. It is the phrase *"mit diesem Kind"* ("with this child") that was troubling. Since the mother had clearly died in childbirth, why did the parson write that it was "with this child?" Of course, the mother could not have died at the birth of a previous or successive child.

On the other hand, perhaps what the parson intended was that the mother had died **together** with this child. If that were the case, perhaps he did not find it necessary to append the notation *"obit"* after the infant Caspar's name. However, the baptismal record does not explicitly use the word "together" (in German, *zusammen*).

This ambiguous phrasing required clarification, but the Sigriswil parish register contains no further evidence. The Caspar Stähli born in 1685 does not appear in a marriage record. Despite the fact that his sister Anna Stähli and her husband Jacob Racheter baptized six children in Sigriswil between 1703 and 1719, Caspar Stähli never served as a witness. Caspar's baptism in 1685 was his sole appearance in the Sigriswil parish records.

Caspar Stähli (1685) did indeed survive—unequivocal proof was eventually found, as I will discuss in the next chapter.

In 1688, Caspar Stähli (d. ca. 1691), now a widower, remarried. Marriage entries in the parish register at the time were very brief, including only the minimal information.

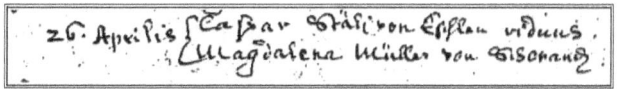

Caspar Stähli, second marriage,
Sigriswil Parish Register, 1688.

The entry reads:

26 April, Caspar Stähli of Aeschlen, widower
Magdalena Müller of Schwanden

This marriage produced two children: Magdalena (1689) and Peter (1691).

The parson who recorded the 1691 baptismal record for Peter appended the suffix "*sel*" after the name of the father, Caspar Stähli (d. ca. 1691). This abbreviation for *selig* indicated that the father had died before the birth of his son.

One of the witnesses at the baptism of Peter Stähli in 1691 was Hans Saurer, designated as "*Alt Reiss Seckelmeister,*" i.e., the former treasurer of the local militia. Most likely, this Hans Saurer was a relative (possibly the father) of the first wife—Benedichta—of Caspar Stähli (d. ca. 1691). This additional instance of a connection between the Saurer family and the Stähli family (not surprising, of course) doesn't, unfortunately, add any clarity to the question of Benedichta Saurer's ancestors.

Magdalena Müller, second wife and widow of Caspar Stähli (d. ca. 1691), was left with two of her own children, both under the age of five, plus three orphaned children from her husband's first marriage: Ulrich, about 14; Anna, about 11; and young Caspar (1685), about 6. How she coped in this difficult situation is not known. I have found no additional marriage record for her, so her circumstances must have been sufficient.

Saurer Family

The lost Sigriswil data from before 1671 makes it impossible to verify Benedichta Saurer's parents. There were two Saurer families at that time, one in Ringoldswil and one in Aeschlen, but I have been unable to determine the precise nature of the connection between the two families.

Ringoldswil, although it belonged to the civil *Gemeinde* Sigriswil, was in the parish of Hilterfingen. Children born in Ringoldswil were baptized in the Hilterfingen parish church (which is located in Oberhofen).

Two Saurer brothers, Michael and Uli (Ulrich), both from Ringoldswil, were (separately) witnesses at the baptism of two sons (Caspar 1673, Ulrich 1677) of Caspar Stähli (d. ca. 1691) and Benedichta Saurer. It was common for siblings of one of the parents to be a witness at a baptism, so this suggests that Benedichta Saurer was a sister to Michael and Uli Saurer. This does not seem to be the case.

Michael Saurer (born 1639) and his brother Uli (born 1647) were the sons of Anthoni Saurer and his wife Anna Saurer. Husband and wife were also second cousins. Between 1629 and 1647, this couple baptized eight children in the Hilterfingen church, producing a baby every 2 or 3 years. Between 1642 and 1647, there is a gap which broke the regular pattern of childbirth for this family. Benedichta Saurer could (in theory) fit into this gap, born between 1644-46. The Hilterfingen parish register does not contain a baptismal record for her in that gap, and although it is possible that the parents baptized her at Sigriswil, it was not the usual procedure. A more likely scenario was that Michael and Uli Saurer were cousins to Benedichta Saurer.

Another possible scenario is that Benedichta Saurer was the daughter of Hans Saurer, the *Alt Reiss Seckelmeister* of Sigriswil. He was a witness at the 1691 baptism of Peter Stähli, as noted above. Hans, the *Seckelmeister,* had several sons who appear to be contemporaries of Benedichta Saurer—they could have been her brothers. This Saurer family resided at Aeschlen, and thus its baptisms were performed in Sigriswil, but the missing data from before 1671 hampers a full understanding of the family.

One other connection is worthwhile to note. A witness at the 1685 baptism of Caspar Stähli was Steffan Boss. He was married to Kathryn Saurer, brother of the infant Christian Saurer, at whose 1653 baptism (in Hilterfingen) a Caspar Stähli was a witness. Was Kathryn Saurer a sister to Benedichta Saurer? I have found no evidence to support this.

No doubt Benedichta Saurer's family (probably living at Aeschlen) was connected, somehow, to the Saurer family living at Ringoldswil. How, exactly, I have not been able to determine. I am not alone in my puzzlement over this. Present-day residents of *Gemeinde* Sigriswil have told me that Saurer family members currently living in the area are aware that there were, at one time, two Saurer families, one at Ringoldswil and one at Aeschlen. However, no one knows what the original connection was.

The Hilterfingen parish register contains Saurer baptisms going back into the middle of the 16th century. Hans Saurer was the parson at the Hilterfingen church from 1595-1600. He was born in 1562 along with his twin brother, Caspar Saurer, who married a Stähli from the Oberhofen clan. Although the Saurer family has been in the area for a long time and remains so today, the mystery persists.

Peter Stähli (1691-1784)

Before I discuss the details of Caspar Stähli (1685) in the next chapter, I must tie up a few loose ends.

Anna Stähli (born 1680), older sister of Caspar Stähli (1685), married Jacob Racheter in 1703, and the couple baptized six children in Sigriswil between 1703 and 1719. Jacob and Anna took over the Stähli homestead and farm in Aeschlen. Descendants remained in Aeschlen until at least the start of the 19th century, although today the Racheter surname seems to have disappeared from the area.

The fate of Magdalena Stähli (born 1689), half-sister of Caspar (1685), is unknown.

Peter Stähli (1691–1764) married Anna Frutiger, and they had one son, Ulli, baptized in 1717. Ulli married Anna Hertig in 1758, and their children, Rosina (born 1760) and Abraham (born 1762), were still very young when their father died from pneumonia in 1766.

Spur Chart 1 (page 38) illustrates Peter Stähli's family and his descendants into the middle of the 19th century.

Abraham Stähli (1762–1813) was the son of Ulli Stähli (1717–1766) and Anna Hertig. Abraham was a member of the Sigriswil *Chorgericht*, a council which was responsible for church discipline. He and his wife, Maria von Gunten, had five children.

In April 1834, Magdalena (born 1792) married Johannes Kämpf, who was 22 years younger. Their child was born in September, 1834. The child did not survive, and Magdalena died in 1845.

Anna (born 1794) married Abraham Tschanz. This couple baptized nine children in Bern (city) between 1818 and 1833, so the family was not living at Sigriswil. When Abraham Tschanz died in 1842, his occupation was noted as a nail smith. Anna Stähli Tschanz died in 1849. This couple's great-grandson emigrated to New York in 1924.

Abraham Stähli's youngest son, Johannes (1795–1829), died from tuberculosis. Ulrich's (born 1789) history is unknown.

Abraham Stähli the younger (1788–1857) married Anna Sauser. Their child, Anna, died in 1842.

Abraham the younger died on board a ship coming from Thun, in 1857, according to the Sigriswil parish records. In this way, the last male Stähli of this line in Sigriswil passed into history upon the waters of the *Thunersee*.

Today, people with the Stähli surname live in *Gemeinde* Sigriswil, but their families originate in other parts of Switzerland. Oberhofen am Thunersee, a few kilometers away, had a large Stähli family that had been there since the early 1500s. That family was not related, on the paternal side, to the Stähli family in Sigriswil.

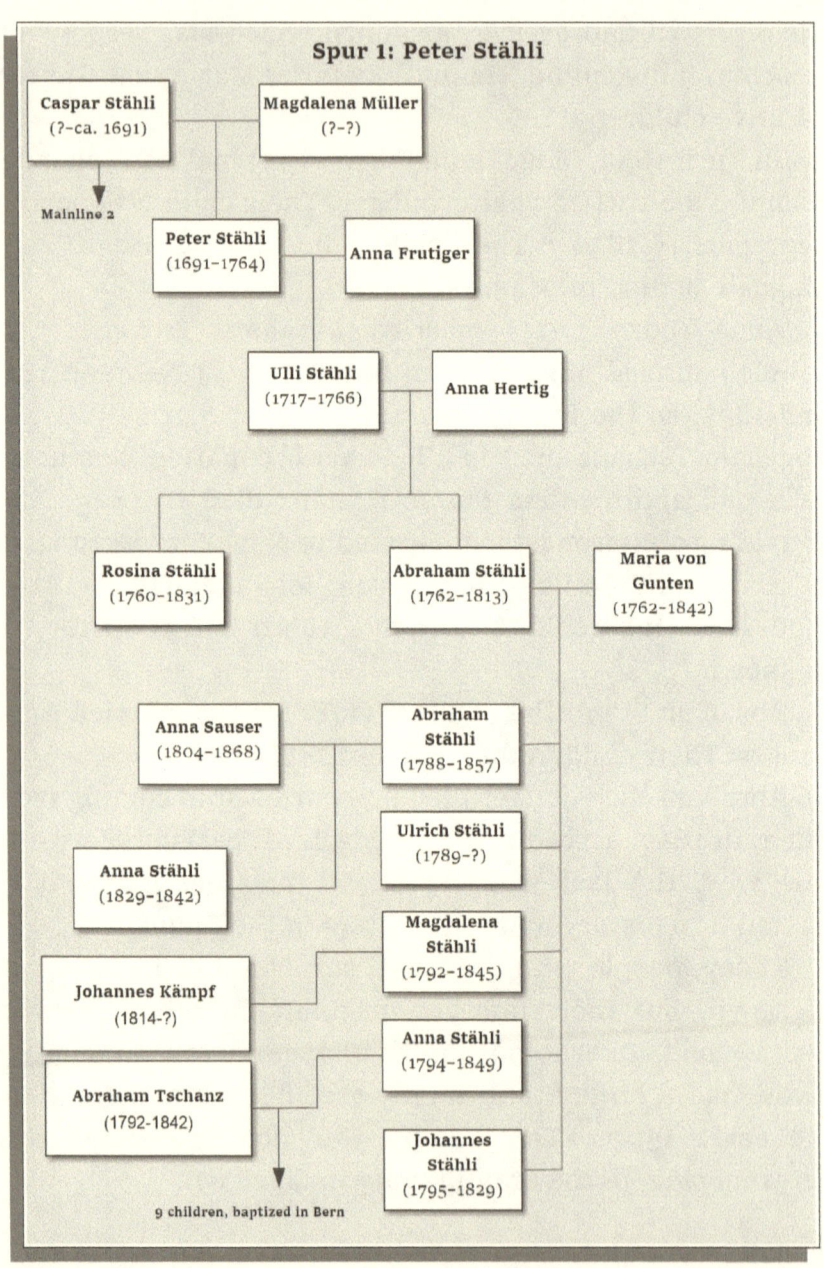

Spur 1: Peter Stähli

Caspar Stähli (?-ca. 1691)

Magdalena Müller (?-?)

Mainline 2

Peter Stähli (1691-1764)

Anna Frutiger

Ulli Stähli (1717-1766)

Anna Hertig

Rosina Stähli (1760-1831)

Abraham Stähli (1762-1813)

Maria von Gunten (1762-1842)

Anna Sauser (1804-1868)

Abraham Stähli (1788-1857)

Ulrich Stähli (1789-?)

Anna Stähli (1829-1842)

Magdalena Stähli (1792-1845)

Johannes Kämpf (1814-?)

Anna Stähli (1794-1849)

Abraham Tschanz (1792-1842)

Johannes Stähli (1795-1829)

9 children, baptized in Bern

2. Into the Pfalz

Sales Contract

As noted earlier, the Sigriswil parish register does not cite Caspar Stähli, born in 1685, at any time after his baptism in March of that year. He was not a witness at the baptisms of any of his nieces and nephews, nor at the baptisms of the children of any of his neighbors. And Caspar does not appear in the marriage register. At that time, young males would typically marry between the age of 25 and 30. A marriage would have been usual anytime after 1705, but the Sigriswil parish register contains no marriage record for him.

This lack of evidence from the parish records could indicate an early death. The Sigriswil death register, however, does not begin until 1748.

Fortunately, two sales contracts from 1713 provide the missing evidence.

The two contracts, discovered in the archives of Canton Bern, show that Caspar, born 1685, survived into adulthood. Although the sales contracts do not explicitly mention emigration, they do provide evidence that a departure was planned.

In their original form, the two contracts were written as one document. The handwriting is difficult—it can be deciphered only by a person experienced in reading such old documents. Archaic forms of land measurement, currency, and the points of the compass are found throughout. For the most part, place names are recognizable, especially to a modern resident of *Gemeinde* Sigriswil.

The two sales contracts were executed on November 18, 1713. They have been slightly edited, translated into English, and names of people and places have been standardized.

Sales Contract (I), 1713

Seller: Caspar Stähli of Aeschlen in the district of Sigriswil.

Buyer: Christoffel Meyer of Ringoldswil.

Property: a meadow, called Rühlboden, situated above Ringoldswil, about ¾ *Juchart* in size, together with the right to use Peter Saurer's barn. The land is bordered on the east by a parcel belonging to Hans Willener of Tschingel; on the south by a parcel belonging to Steffan Frutiger (where access to the parcel is also located); and on the north by a parcel belonging to Uli Saurer. Everything pertaining to the land is included, including the harvest from this year...free of taxes and encumbrances...

Purchase Price: 60 kroner, which consists of 56 kroner for the piece of land, and 5 kroner for a gratuity. Received in cash and receipted...all done properly and according to form...

Witnesses: Johannes Heinrich Blösch; Jacob Racheter of Aeschlen, the seller's brother-in-law; Hans Willener of Tschingel; Jacob Spihlmann of Hilterfingen.

18 November 1713

Sales Contract (II), 1713

Seller: Caspar Stähli of Aeschlen in the district of Sigriswil.

Buyer: Jacob Racheter of Aeschlen—the seller's brother-in-law.

Property: All property and communal rights pertaining to his house, home and farmstead, which the seller inherited from his late parents, and which is well-known to both buyer and seller.

Property: A parcel of vineyard of 15 *Klafter* at Amsoldingen in the district of Sigriswil, bordered on the east by a parcel belonging to Barbara Saurer.

Property: Another parcel of vineyard of 6 *Klafter* located in the Ey, in the district of Sigriswil, bordered on the east by a parcel belonging to Hans von Gunten, bordered on the south by the Eygraben, access to the parcel is from Hans von Gunten's parcel, bordered on the north by a parcel belonging to the late Hans Stähli, the seller's brother. Includes all rights to the community grape press on the road to Amsoldingen. Free of taxes and encumbrances. Includes the land, 20 casks of wine, and half of this year's grape harvest.

Purchase Price: 15 kroner. Received in cash and receipted... all done properly and according to form...

Witnesses: Johannes Heinrich Blösch; Christoffel and Hans Meyer—brothers, of Ringoldswil.

18 November 1713

The first contract transfers a parcel of meadowland in Ringoldswil to the buyer. The parcel was situated somewhere above the tiny hamlet of Ringoldswil. The word used in the contract for the parcel is *Mattland,* which is the Swiss term for a meadow or a pasture. The land may have been used for pasturing cows or calves, for growing grain, or for growing grasses to be made into hay for the winter months when the cows were brought down from the upper Alpine pastures, where they would typically spend the summer. The size of the parcel is given as ¾ *Juchart,* which in modern terms is approximately one acre. A *Juchart* is an archaic form of land measurement which roughly approximated the amount of ground a team of horses could plow in one day—typically about 1.5 acres.

The sale included the use of a barn, presumably nearby, belonging to Peter Saurer, and the sale also included the harvest from the current year. What this harvest, in November, might have been is not known—perhaps hay or grain stored in the barn.

The borders of the parcel are specified by describing the adjacent parcels and their owner. However, instead of using the usual directional notation—north, south, east and west, the original document used the German terms *Mitternacht (*midnight, i.e, north*); Mittag* (noon, south); *Sonnenaufgang* (sunrise, east); *Sonnenuntergang* (sunset, west). How the parcel was accessed is explicitly stated.

The parcel was sold for 60 kroner. Whether that was a large sum or small, in today's terms, is not known.

It is probable that Caspar Stähli inherited the parcel of meadowland from his mother, Benedichta Saurer. The parcel is bordered on one side by a parcel belonging to a Uli Saurer, and the barn of Peter Saurer was also nearby.

These two men were likely uncles or cousins of Caspar Stähli, the seller. They might have been brothers of his mother, or more likely, descendants of brothers of his mother.

The second sales contract transfers three pieces of property from Caspar Stähli, the seller, to the buyer, his brother-in-law, Jacob Racheter. The property was his house and farm, and two parcels of vineyard.

The house and farm are described as having been inherited from Caspar's late parents. The exact location is not specified; rather, the contract states that the location was well-known to both seller and buyer—as it would be in a such a tiny community.

Sold along with the house were all rights pertaining to it. The exact Swiss term used is *Rechtsame*, an untranslatable word that means, approximately, "all those rights and privileges which pertain to a citizen and property owner in this location." This might include such things as rights to common grazing land, rights to harvest firewood from common woodland, rights to use water from a certain stream, or use of community owned machinery, such as a grist mill. The fact that Caspar Stähli gave up all the benefits of local citizenship strongly indicates that he planned to leave Sigriswil.

The two pieces of vineyard are described with the archaic term *Klafter*. This term measured the distance between two out-stretched arms of an adult. How this one-dimensional unit of measure was used to define the two-dimensional size of a vineyard is puzzling. Perhaps each vineyard parcel consisted of a single row of grapes.

The first parcel of vineyard was at "Amsoldingen in the district of Sigriswil." This is confusing, since Amsoldingen is a town southwest of Thun, and is not in the district of Sigriswil. However, a large area of vineyards, extending downhill from Ringoldswil and almost reaching the shore of the lake, belonged at one time to the collegiate church of St. Mauritius at Amsoldingen. After the Reformation, most of this church-owned property passed to private owners or to Canton Bern.

By 1713, the vineyards named "Amsoldingen" in the district of Sigriswil were in private hands, but the area was still referred to by its traditional name. Caspar Stähli's parcel, consisting of 15 *Klafter,* was adjacent to that of Barbara Saurer, who was likely another of his maternal relatives.

The large area of vineyards known as Amsoldingen is still present today, although the area is used primarily for orchards and pasture. A satellite image of Ringoldswil and its surroundings shows a large area south of the cluster houses that make up the hamlet. Bordered on two sides by woodland, the open area extends down the very steep slope toward the lake, to Oertli.

The second parcel of vineyard is in Aeschlen itself. It references place names that still exist today. The parcel was situated on the steep, south-facing slopes directly below Aeschlen, nestled between two areas of wetland. On the north, this parcel bordered that of Hans Stähli, the "seller's late brother." I have never found any other reference to this person. He was born, apparently, before the church fire of 1671, and may have resided elsewhere, as the Sigriswil parish register does not cite him in any way.

The sale of the vineyard parcels included the right to use the community grape press, located near the

Amsoldingen vineyards. It also included 20 casks of wine, and half of the current year's grape harvest.

The price for these three parcels was 15 kroner. Considering that this included the house, farm, and two vineyards, this seems to me to be a small amount when compared to the 60 kroner that Caspar Stähli received for the meadow in Ringoldswil. Perhaps, as Caspar sold these parcels to his brother-in-law, in the family, he did not ask the price he might have received from a third party buyer.

The crucial piece of information from these sales contracts is that Jacob Racheter was explicitly identified as the seller's brother-in-law (in German, *Schwager*). Together, the sales contracts and the Sigriswil parish register for the 1703 marriage of Anna Stähli and Jacob Racheter prove that Caspar Stähli (born 1685) had indeed survived.

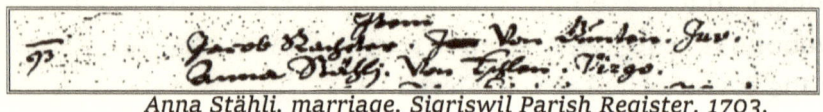
Anna Stähli, marriage, Sigriswil Parish Register, 1703.

The record reads:

Jacob Racheter, of Gunten, Juv[enus]
Anna Stähli, of Aeschlen, Virgo

The Latin terms "*Juvenus*" and "*Virgo*" indicate that the bride and groom had not previously been married: literally "young man" and "virgin." Gunten, one of the eleven villages belonging to *Gemeinde* Sigriswil, is situated directly below Aeschlen, on the shore of the *Thunersee*.

Reasons for Leaving

The sales contracts provide strong evidence that Caspar Stähli intended to leave Switzerland, and that he intended never to reside in Sigriswil again. By the end of 1714, Caspar Stähli, born 1685, had relocated to the Pfalz (German Palatinate), had married, and had a son. How and why did this happen? No explicit reasons are given in the sales contract—I can only speculate.

One of the reasons for leaving could have been economic, i.e., the search for better economic conditions outside of Switzerland.

After the Thirty Years' War (1618–1648) had devastated and depopulated the Pfalz, the ruling princes and electors there had invited Swiss immigrants to settle.

The Thirty Years' War had started as a dispute between Protestant and Catholic ruling factions, and had ended as a very bloody, extremely destructive struggle between France and the Hapsburg Empire for supremacy in Europe. Successive armies invaded the area between the Rhine River (in the east) and the French border (in the west). Entire districts were plundered, and much of the population had either been killed, had starved, died of disease, or had simply moved elsewhere.

After the Peace of Westphalia ended hostilities in 1648, the Protestant princes in the Pfalz sought to repopulate their estates using Swiss immigrants. Switzerland had remained neutral in the war, but economic conditions there apparently made emigration into the Pfalz an attractive option. Large families in combination with a limited amount of arable land may have been contributing factors. Many of the Protestant princes in the Pfalz belonged to the Reformed Church, and doubtless this appealed to prospective Swiss settlers, who also belonged to the Reformed branch of Protestantism, for the most part. Today, the existence of Swiss surnames in parts of Rheinland-Pfalz testifies to the success of the immigration project.

Was this Caspar Stähli's motivation? I do not find it very plausible. In the first place, he emigrated in 1713/14, after the initial waves of emigration following the war. In addition, he was one of the lucky few who actually possessed a house, a farm, and other property in Sigriswil. Caspar Stähli was not a landless younger son, forced into emigration to make his way in the world.

On the other hand, I cannot, of course, know the exact nature of his economic circumstances either in Sigriswil or in the Pfalz. It is not obvious to me that Caspar Stähli's economic situation in the Pfalz had been improved by his relocation. He was an itinerant journeyman, someone who acquired work on a short-term basis on various estates around the district of Kaiserslautern. The births of his children in different localities in this area suggest an unsettled existence for his family, although this was probably not unusual.

Caspar Stähli's elder brother Ulrich had moved to the Pfalz in 1701, as the note in the Sigriswil parish register indicates. Although Ulrich's further history is unknown, the brothers may have remained in touch, and Ulrich's circumstances in the Pfalz encouraged the younger brother to make a similar move. Although this is certainly possible, I have found no evidence for it.

Another consideration was that of marriage. At some point, Caspar Stähli married Magdalena Schedeberger.[1] I have been unable to determine where this occurred, but perhaps it was on a scouting visit to the Pfalz, and as a result Caspar decided to leave Switzerland to join his new wife in a new place. This is also speculation: I have no evidence.

Religion was probably the biggest factor in Caspar Stähli's decision to emigrate. Although there is no explicit evidence that Caspar belonged to an Anabaptist sect in Switzerland, the circumstances suggest that he did, or was at least sympathetic. This would be ample reason for emigration to the Pfalz.

The Anabaptist Movement

The roots of the Anabaptist movement in Switzerland can be traced back to about 1520 and Ulrich Zwingli's brand of Protestantism in the city of Zürich. The more extreme reformers thought that Zwingli was rejecting one state-dominated Christian church (the Roman Catholic), for another, the new Protestant establishment. These radical reformers asserted the primacy of the Bible, and the right of an adult to make his or her own choices about matters of religion, without interference from governmental or ecclesiastical hierarchies. Similar

---

1 It is not certain that "Schedeberger" is the correct surname for Caspar Stähli's wife. Except for one instance, the baptismal and confirmation records of the couple's children omit the mother's surname. Only at the baptism of Caspar and Magdalena's son Ulrich, in Hochspeyer in 1726, is the mother's surname noted—it is written as "Schleberger." In the same record, Magdalena is identified as an Anabaptist. Most German genealogists have apparently decided, for unknown reasons, that the correct surname was "Schedeberger."

movements were taking place in other parts of Europe. Despite severe persecution from both Catholic and Protestant factions, the movement took hold among a few people, especially in the Netherlands and Switzerland.

The Anabaptist movement found particularly fertile ground in Canton Bern—in the Emmental, and around the shores of the *Thunersee*.

From the beginning, the Bernese cantonal government took a harsh view of the non-conformist religious sect. Punitive mandates, fines, appropriation of property, imprisonment, and sentences of death or a life of servitude as a galley slave were among the measures for anyone openly practicing Anabaptist beliefs.[2]

Some of the objections of the Bernese government were the Anabaptists' rejection of infant baptism, their refusal to bear arms or swear oaths of allegiance, and their refusal to regularly attend the services of the state-sanctioned Reformed Church. The cantonal government viewed these as dire threats to the established order, and it strictly punished transgressors.

There was a particularly harsh program of persecution in 1670/71, when many Bernese Anabaptists left for Alsace, for the German Pfalz, for the Jura Mountains, or for Neuchâtel, which at that time was not part of the Swiss Confederation.

Another wave of persecution in the early 1690s sent yet more Anabaptists into exile in Alsace or the Pfalz. In Steffisburg, a town on the *Thunersee* a few kilometers from Sigriswil, Anabaptist families disappeared in the 1690s, including those with such well-known names as

---

2   See page 18. The term, "Anabaptist," which was formerly pejorative, means "one who baptizes again." It is equivalent to the German term "*Wiedertäufer*.

Joder, Kauffmann and Zimmermann. These families later surfaced in Alsace and in the area in Germany west of the Rhine River.

These measures were not totally effective: some Anabaptists stayed behind, either in hiding or remaining unobtrusive, depending on the silence of their neighbors to keep them safe from the reach of the cantonal government.

In 1711, the Bernese government undertook a new scheme: deportation of the renegade Anabaptists. Coreligionists and a sympathetic government in the Netherlands agreed to accept the exiles, and arrangements were made to place the deportees on ships that would carry them down the Rhine.

Were there Anabaptists living at Sigriswil? Several families from *Gemeinde* Sigriswil were among the 1711 exiles. One of the family members, Hans Rupp, from Gunten, was imprisoned for his Anabaptist beliefs in 1709, on an island in the middle of the Aare River, in the city of Bern. A year later, he was one of the prisoners in a failed scheme of forced exile to Carolina in North America. After the prisoners were freed at Nijmegen, in the Netherlands, they visited a nearby Mennonite congregation at Kleve. Then, apparently, Hans Rupp made his way back to his family in Switzerland.

The Sigriswil parish register notes that when several of Hans Rupp's children were presented for baptism, shortly after birth, the father was designated as an Anabaptist. Usually, in such cases, the child was presented for baptism by another male relative.

Hans Rupp and his brother Christian Rupp, along with their wives and children, were among the exiles to the

Netherlands. Also exiled were Maria Rupp (Hans and Christian's sister) and her husband, Ulrich Brunner.

Another family, Hans Frutiger and his wife, Maria Kämpf, of Aeschlen, were also exiled to the Netherlands. Both individuals, who were certainly close neighbors with Caspar Stähli, were designated as Anabaptists at the Sigriswil baptisms of their children.

One of the witnesses at the 1705 baptism of Hans Frutiger's son was Hans Baur of Oberhofen, who married Anna Willener, from Sigriswil. This couple was also exiled in 1711.

Hans Frutiger was imprisoned in Bern in July, 1710. The circumstances surrounding his arrest are not known. Hans' father, Ulrich, was also exiled, along with his wife and children.

So it is clear that there were Anabaptists at Sigriswil at the time. Certainly they would have been known to each other and to Caspar Stähli. One of the strategies that Anabaptists used to avoid detection was to consider themselves *"Halbtäufer,"* i.e., "half baptist"—one who sympathized with the beliefs of the Anabaptists but outwardly conformed to the strictures of the Reformed Church.

Of course, in 1713, Caspar Stähli would have been aware of what happened to his neighbors a few years before. Since confiscation of property was one of the penalties sometimes exacted on Anabaptists by the Bernese government, he may have decided to sell out and emigrate when he could, under his own terms, without suffering financial penalties.

Perhaps he was *Halbtäufer*, or his soon-to-be-wife Magdalena was an Anabaptist. It is clear that the Caspar

Stähli-Magdalena Schedeberger family was connected, somehow, with the Anabaptist community in the Pfalz.

The emigration of Caspar Stähli (born 1685) probably occurred for these religious reasons. Of course, it need not have been so simple: a combination of economic, personal and religious reasons could certainly have been the motivating factors. Caspar Stähli left Sigriswil sometime after November 18, 1713, and so far as is known, never went back.

*

Mainline Chart 3 (page 54) illustrates the family of Caspar Stähli and Magdalena Schedeberger, as it was in the Pfalz. The birth years of their children were extracted from baptismal records (except for Eva Catharina). Although the marriage record for Caspar and Magdalena has never been located, I assume that the marriage took place in the Pfalz, as there is no record of Magdalena in the Sigriswil parish register. The unknown origin of the surname "Schedeberger" hampers research into her heritage.

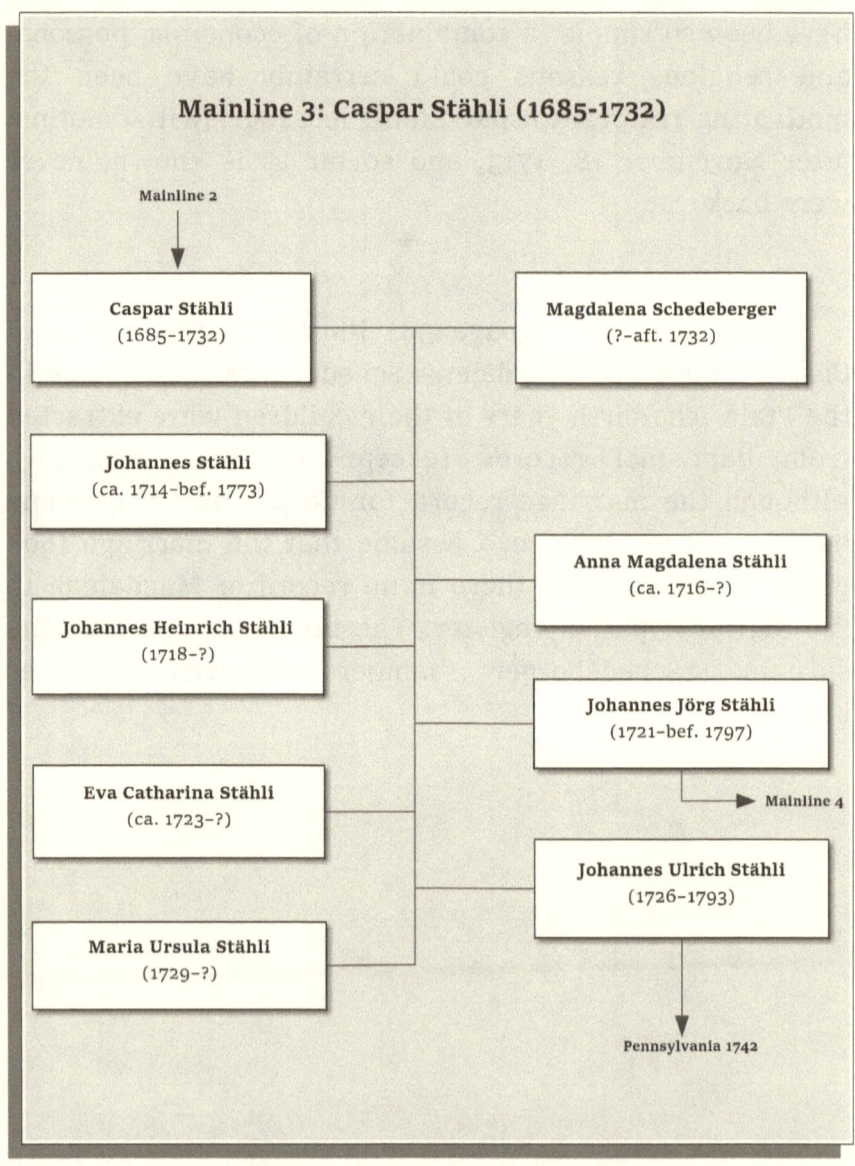

Mainline 3: Caspar Stähli (1685-1732)

Mainline 2

Caspar Stähli
(1685-1732)

Magdalena Schedeberger
(?-aft. 1732)

Johannes Stähli
(ca. 1714-bef. 1773)

Anna Magdalena Stähli
(ca. 1716-?)

Johannes Heinrich Stähli
(1718-?)

Johannes Jörg Stähli
(1721-bef. 1797)

Mainline 4

Eva Catharina Stähli
(ca. 1723-?)

Johannes Ulrich Stähli
(1726-1793)

Maria Ursula Stähli
(1729-?)

Pennsylvania 1742

The *Pfälzerwald*

Where Caspar Stähli first resided when he left Switzerland for the Pfalz is not known. Nor is it known where he married his wife, Magdalena Schedeberger (as she will be called here).

What is known is that a son, Johannes, was born in 1714. In July 1718, Johannes Stähli and his sister Anna were baptized in the Reformed church at Waldfischbach, which is situated about 20 kilometers southwest of Kaiserslautern, in Rheinland-Pfalz, as the area is now called in modern Germany. In the baptismal record from the Waldfischbach parish register, Johannes' age was given as 4 years; his sister Anna was 2.

The baptismal register reads:

> *July 3, 1718. Caspar Stähli, a Swiss man from the Sigriswil district under the jurisdiction of Bern, now keeping himself at Aschbacherhof, and his wife Magdalena, belonging to the Anabaptist religion, presented two children for baptism, a son aged 4 years, and a daughter aged 2, named Johannes and Anna Magdalena. Witnesses: Johannes Teutscher from Stelzenberg, Johannes Müllener from Saanen in Switzerland, and Anna Elsbeth Teutscher.*

It is somewhat surprising to me to find the children of Anabaptist parents being baptized in a Reformed church. It is true that the children were no longer infants, but neither were Johannes and Anna adults, and able to make their own religious decisions — one of the principal tenets of Anabaptist belief.

The original baptismal entry from the Waldfischbach parish register does not make clear whether **both** parents belonged to an Anabaptist sect. The German grammar leaves open to interpretation whether only the mother, Magdalena, was an Anabaptist, or Caspar Stähli, the father, was Anabaptist as well. The fact that several years had elapsed since the births of the children would suggest that both parents were Anabaptist, since the Reformed Church required that newborns be baptized as soon as possible after birth.

Most likely, however, the baptisms were performed *pro forma*, i.e., done in compliance with local regulations, so that the family could continue to live without problems in the community, and to preserve rights of citizenship. Law under some of the German principalities at the time required that residents register with one of the approved churches (Catholic, Reformed, Lutheran), even though the law did not necessarily mandate regular attendance. The Amish-Mennonite church was not an approved church.

Aschbacherhof, mentioned in the baptismal record, is a farming estate south of Kaiserslautern. Like other farms of the period, it was typical in that it consisted of a group of buildings surrounding a courtyard (the *Hof*). The estate was originally in the hands of the Flersheim family, one of whose members was the Bishop of Speyer. Tenants, leaseholders, and their families, supplemented by others, were responsible for working the surrounding fields, which were likely extensive.

After the Thirty Years' War, the landowners, along with others in the area, had encouraged Swiss immigrants to settle on their estates to return the land to productive use.

It was a mutually beneficial situation: the landowners derived income from the lease of the land and from its produce; the Swiss immigrants, including Anabaptists, received a portion of the produce of the land as well as promises of (limited) religious freedom and rights of citizenship.

Aschbacherhof remains standing today, surrounded by fields in the hills and woodland of the *Pfälzerwald,* the band of upland forest that stretches from Enkenbach in the north to the French border in the south. Adjacent to the present day *Hof* buildings are the ruins of the church of St. Blasius. The *Pfälzerwald* (see page 59) was a favored place of residence for Anabaptists, perhaps because of its isolation.

Ruins of St. Blasius at Aschbacherhof

In November 1718, Caspar Stähli and his wife baptized another son, Johannes Heinrich,[3] in the church at Trippstadt, a few kilometers from the Aschbacherhof. In 1719, ownership of the Aschbacherhof passed to Ludwig Anton von Hacke, whose family later built a palatial mansion at Trippstadt.

By 1721, the Stähli family was living at Diemerstein, a hamlet hidden deep in a woodland valley. Diemerstein would remain the family's principal place of residence until emigration to the United States in 1835.

Caspar Stähli and his wife Magdalena had four additional children: Johannes Jörg (1721); Eva Catharina (about 1723); Johannes Ulrich (1726); Maria Ursula (1729).

The varied locations of the baptisms of the children hint at an unsettled life for the family. The first two children were baptized in the church at Waldfischbach. Heinrich, the third child, was baptized in the church at Trippstadt. The next son, Hans-Jörg (as he will be known in this history), was baptized at Diemerstein, and the baptism was recorded in the Sembach parish register. The birth circumstances of Eva Catharina are not known. Johannes Ulrich was born in Diemerstein and baptized in the Hochspeyer church, a few kilometers away. And the last child, Maria Ursula, was born at Heltersberg and baptized in the church at Waldfischbach. All of these churches belonged to the Reformed branch of Protestantism, except for the Hochspeyer church, which was Lutheran.

---

3   In Germany, each son in a family was sometimes given the first name of Johannes; each daughter was named Maria. Apparently, the child's second (middle) name was the one used in everyday life.

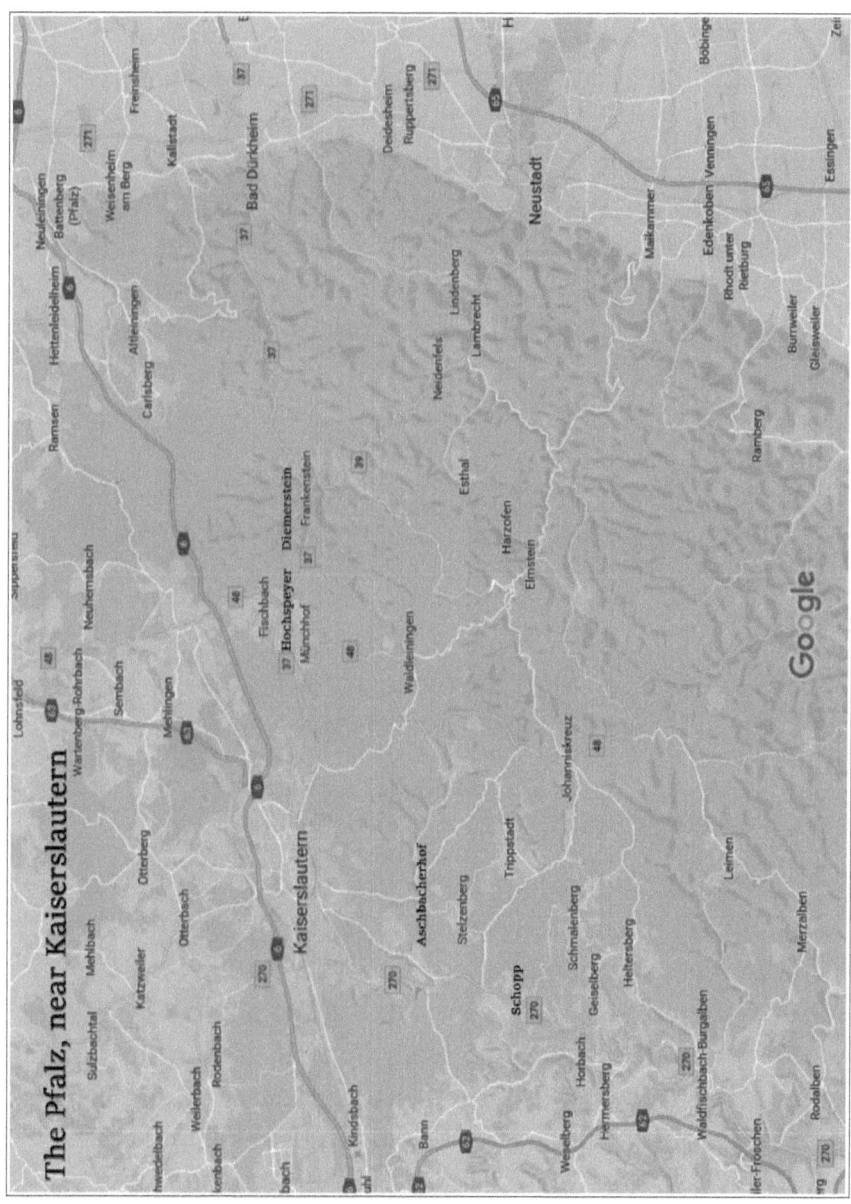

The Pfalz, near Kaiserslautern

The locations of each of these baptisms were not, in relative terms, very far from each other, but the varied locations do suggest that Caspar Stähli and his family moved from farming estate to estate, taking work where he could find it. Apparently, he specialized in pigs, since, in several of these baptismal records, Caspar Stähli, the children's father, is designated as a *Hirt* or *Schweinehirt*, i.e., a tender of swine.

Caspar Stähli died at Schopp, a small village southwest of Kaiserslautern, in May 1732. The death entry does not record a cause of death, but it does contain several pieces of crucial information.

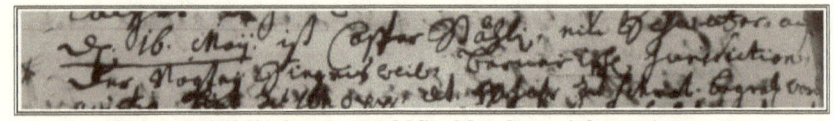

Caspar Stähli, death, Waldfischbach Parish Register, 1732.

This entry is very difficult to decipher. The English translation has been slightly abridged:

> *May 16, [1732] Caspar Stähli a Swiss man from Sigriswil in the jurisdiction of Bern, died, aged 47 years...*

Caspar Stähli seems fated to cause family researchers challenges in researching the details of his life. His ambiguous baptismal record from 1685 called into question whether he even survived his birth. His death record, while providing very useful information that connected him with Sigriswil, appears to be a little perplexing in terms of the age given at the time of death.

Family researchers know that death notices and obituaries are notoriously unreliable. They are typically provided by a surviving family member, who may or may not have accurate and/or complete information. In this case, the person who wrote the death entry in the Waldfischbach parish register was, apparently, uncertain what Caspar Stähli's age was at the time of his death.

Examining the last line of the entry, in the middle of the script, the word "Jahre"—"years"—can barely be discerned. Directly before this word, the number "40" appears to be written, with the numeric "0" being overwritten by a "7". Or, was the "7" overwritten by a "0"? Thus, Caspar's age at his death was either 47 years, or 40 years. 1732 minus 47 years computes to a birth year of 1685, which matches precisely the year of his baptism found in the Sigriswil parish register. 1732 minus 40 computes to a birth year of 1692, in which year no Caspar Stähli was baptized in Sigriswil. The perfect match of name, place and birth year seems too good to ignore, so an age at death of 47 is assumed to be correct.

In September 1732, Magdalena Schedeberger, Caspar Stähli's widow, married Caspar Mader in Horbach, a hamlet very near to the various locations where the Stähli family had lived since 1714. The parish register of the Catholic church in Horbach records (in Latin) the wedding on September 9, 1732, adding a comment that the bride Magdalena was from the Anabaptist sect, and had converted to the "true religion."

It may appear surprising that the widow, Magdalena, remarried less than four months after the death of her first husband, Caspar Stähli. However, it must be remembered that women of that era had few options if they were lacking adequate financial resources. Magdalena had seven children under the age of 20, if they had all survived. A widow with young children would be obligated to remarry, and quickly, if she wanted to ensure that her children did not starve.

Likewise, a man who lost a wife and with young children still at home would have found it necessary to acquire a wife fairly quickly. For reasons of propriety, a widowed man could not have a woman (who was not his wife) in the household to keep house for himself and his children. And yet, without someone to mind the children, prepare food, etc., the man could not work outside the home to provide for his family. Remarriage for a widowed man or woman with young children was a practical and economic imperative. It is not surprising that Magdalena remarried so soon. Whether Caspar Mader, her new husband, also had young children from an earlier marriage is not known.

The Question of Religion

The exact religious status of the Caspar Stähli-Magdalena Schedeberger family during these early years in the Pfalz is not altogether clear. The evidence suggests that Caspar Stähli left Switzerland because he was an Anabaptist, or perhaps he was a *Halbtäufer,* an Anabaptist sympathizer. As the origins of his wife are not known, her religious affiliation is likewise obscure. The 1718 baptisms of their children, Johannes and Anna, identify Magdalena as an Anabaptist, as does the 1726 baptism of son Ulrich. And, as noted above, Magdalena, at her second marriage in 1732, was described as having been an Anabaptist, although she had converted to Catholicism at some point.

The German grammar of the baptismal record for the children Johannes and Anna in 1718 is ambiguous on whether Caspar Stähli was also Anabaptist. The baptismal records of the other children, Johannes Heinrich (1718), Hans-Jörg (1721), and Maria Ursula (1729), are silent on the question of the parents' religion. The baptismal record of Eva has not been found.

It is possible that Caspar was the "true believer" in Anabaptist tenets, and his wife Magdalena had, as a matter of course, gone along. Since she had converted to Catholicism by the time she married her second husband, perhaps she tended to go along with the beliefs of her spouse, in order to secure the economic and social benefits of marriage.

A last piece of evidence is entirely unambiguous. In May 1733, Eva Catharina Stähli converted to Catholicism, according to an entry in the Horbach parish register. In that entry, Eva is designated as being "the daughter of the Swiss Anabaptist, Caspar Stähli."

Ultimately, it is the life of Hans-Jörg Stähli that provides the evidence which indicates that Anabaptist traditions within the family persisted into the following generations, and were carried across the Atlantic Ocean over 100 years later.

Children of Caspar and Magdalena

Very is little is known about five of the seven children of Caspar and Magdalena.

Johannes Stähli (born circa 1714) was baptized in 1718 in the church at Waldfischbach, and confirmed in 1733 in the same church (along with his sister, Anna, and brother,

Johannes Heinrich). Whether these confirmations were undertaken to comply with local requirements or for other reasons is not known.

Johannes died sometime before 1773. When Johannes' widow, Anna Eva, died in 1773 in Schmalenberg, she was noted as having a son (name unknown) who survived. The surname of Johannes' wife is likewise not known.

As noted, **Anna Magdalena Stähli** (born circa 1716) and **Johannes Heinrich Stähli** (born 1718) were confirmed in 1733 in Waldfischbach.

Johannes Jörg Stähli (born 1721) is discussed in more detail in the following section.

Eva Catharina Stähli (birth date unknown) converted to the Roman Catholic faith in 1733. No other details are known.

Johannes Ulrich Stähli (born 1726) emigrated to Pennsylvania in 1742, aboard the ship *Francis and Elizabeth*. He was about 16 years old, and most likely traveled as a redemptioner or indentured servant. His name ("Uhllerich Ställy") on the passenger list among the list of 13 Amish-Mennonite adult men on the ship suggests that he was acquainted with some among them. It is possible that he had been working with them on one of the farming estates near Schopp, where he was probably living. Wilensteinerhof is one possibility. The three Zug brothers and their stepfather, Jacob Guth, were living there prior to their emigration on the *Francis and Elizabeth*. Aschbacherhof, where Johannes Ulrich's father had worked years before, is also a possibility.

In Pennsylvania, Ulrich Steely (as the name came to be written) purchased 100 acres of land in 1770, in

Cumberland (now Mifflin) County. When Ulrich died in 1793, he left behind four sons and three daughters.

Maria Ursula Stähli, Caspar and Magdalena's youngest child, was born in 1729. Nothing else is known of her life.

Hans-Jörg Stähli

The Sembach parish register documents the birth of Hans-Jörg Stähli in 1721 in Diemerstein.

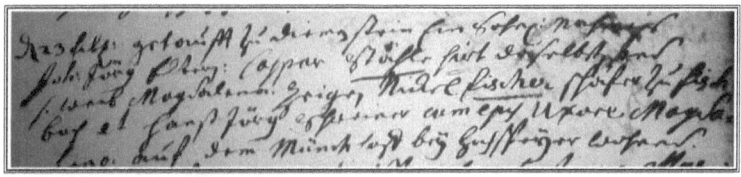

Johannes Jörg Stähli, baptism, Sembach Parish Register, 1721.

The transcription is:[4]

> *1721 den 23 Fbr: getauft zu Diemerstein ein Sohn: nahmens Joh. Jörg. Eltern: Caspar Stähle Hirt daselbst und seine Weib Magdalena. Zeugen Michel Fischer, Schäfer zu Fischbach et Hans Jörg Schreier cum ejus uxore Magdalena auf dem Münchhof bei Hochspeyer wohnend.*

---

4 An interesting etymological aside: the German in this baptismal entry uses two different words for "shepherd." The first, *Hirt*, referring to Caspar Stähli, is similar to the English word "herder." The second, *Schäfer*, referring to one of the witnesses, is derived from the German word for a sheep, "*Schaf.*" In other contexts, Caspar Stähli is referred to as a *Schweinehirt*, i.e., a tender of swine. This term is clearly similar to the archaic English term "swineherd" and is also comparable to the English word "cowherd." A *Schäfer* is what English speakers call someone who tends sheep, i.e, a shepherd, or, in the old form, "sheep-herd."

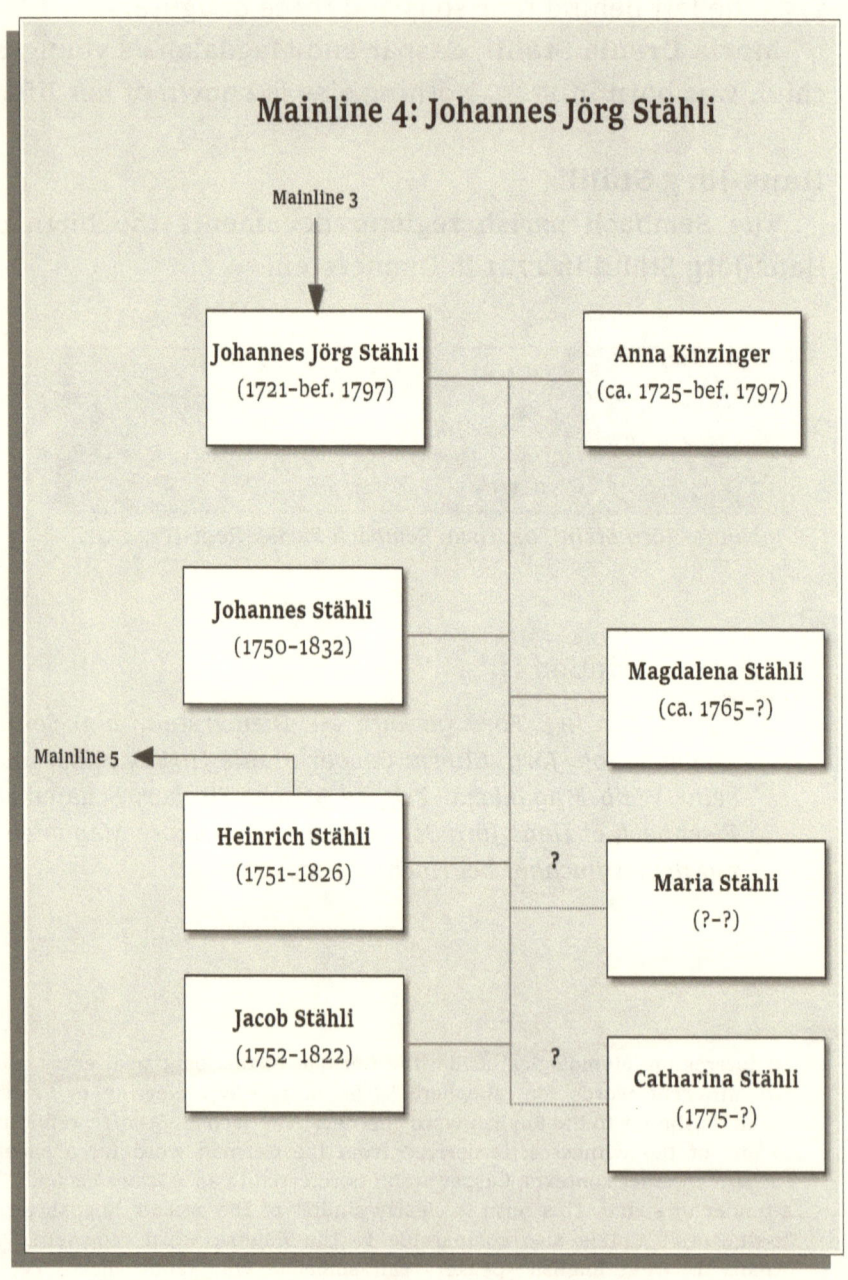

Mainline 4: Johannes Jörg Stähli

Mainline 3

Johannes Jörg Stähli
(1721-bef. 1797)

Anna Kinzinger
(ca. 1725-bef. 1797)

Johannes Stähli
(1750-1832)

Magdalena Stähli
(ca. 1765-?)

Mainline 5

Heinrich Stähli
(1751-1826)

?

Maria Stähli
(?-?)

Jacob Stähli
(1752-1822)

?

Catharina Stähli
(1775-?)

Although the entry seems to indicate that the baptism of Hans-Jörg Stähli occurred at Diemerstein, I question whether this can be correct. There was no church at Diemerstein, and even if the baptism somehow took place there, why was it recorded in the Sembach parish register?

The church at Sembach was part of the Reformed denomination, i.e., one of the state-approved denominations for registering infant births. Later, a Mennonite community was established at Sembach, where it survives to the present day. It would make sense if the child Hans-Jörg Stähli was born at Diemerstein and was baptized at Sembach, so perhaps the parson made an error.

Mainline Chart 4 (page 66) illustrates the family of Hans-Jörg Stähli (who is called by his full name, Johannes Jörg Stähli, on the chart). At some point before 1750, he married Anna Kinzinger.

I have not been able to find the marriage record. Nor have I found the birth records of any of the couple's children. The birth years (when known) have been computed from the marriage or death records of the couple's children.

Very few details are known about the lives of Hans-Jörg Stähli and Anna Kinzinger. The parish register of the Mennonite church at Sembach recorded, in 1797, the marriage of Heinrich Stähli (born 1751) to Anna Widmer. In that record, there are brief notations about Heinrich's parents. Hans-Jörg is described as being from Diemerstein, and as a *"Taglöhner,"* i.e., a journeyman (day laborer), who was hired on a short-term basis for farm work. In this record, Hans-Jörg is called "Georg"—a modern version of the name "Jörg." The record also indicates that Hans-Jörg Stähli had died in Freinsheim, but the year of death is not stated.

Freinsheim is situated about 25 kilometers west and north of Diemerstein, east of the *Pfälzerwald,* and on the flat lands of the Rhine plain. Johannes Stähli (born 1750), eldest son of Hans-Jörg Stähli, married a woman from Freinsheim, so it is likely that the family resided there for a time. A nearby congregation at Friedelsheim served the Mennonites living at Freinsheim.

Today, the ancient, walled village of Freinsheim is surrounded by vineyards.

Anna Kinzinger is described in her son's marriage record as having died at Annweiler, much further south in the *Pfälzerwald.* Again, age and death year are not specified.

At least three of the children (Heinrich, Jacob, Magdalena) of Hans-Jörg and Anna Kinzinger took marriage partners with known Amish-Mennonite connections.[5] Thus, it is highly probable that the Stähli-Kinzinger family was connected to the Amish-Mennonite community in the Pfalz at that time. It was usual for Amish-Mennonites to marry within their own community of co-believers.

Indeed, Hans-Jörg Stähli himself apparently married a woman from an Amish-Mennonite family. Künzi/Kinzinger was a family of Swiss immigrants with Amish-Mennonite connections who lived at Diemerstein.

---

5   At this point, I begin to use the term "Amish-Mennonite" instead of the more general term "Anabaptist." See page 18. "Mennonite" and "Amish" are derived from Menno Simons, a former priest in the Netherlands who was an influential religious reformer, and Jacob Ammann, a Swiss leader in the Anabaptist movement.

Künzi/Kinzinger

In 1687, Peter Künzi, a Mennonite from Buchholterberg, Canton Bern, took over the lease of a broken down mill in the village of Diemerstein. The lease of the mill was purchased from Marie von Oranien, a Dutch princess who had married Ludwig Heinrich Moritz von Simmern, in Kleve.

He was count (*Pfalzgraf*) and duke (*Herzog*) of Simmern and Kaiserslautern. The count had died in 1674, so his widow Marie—the princess and *Pfalzgräfin*— apparently had control of the property. When Peter Künzi bought the lease of the mill, the contract specifically granted him freedom of religion, noting that it would be equivalent to those freedoms enjoyed by the people on the neighboring Fischbacherhof.

Peter Künzi was born in 1652, in Buchholterberg, in the parish of Diessbach (today, Oberdiessbach), in Canton Bern. Spur Chart 2 (page 70) shows this family along with a descent to Anna Kinzinger. Some of the data on this chart is speculative, as no firm connection has been established between the Peter Künzi who was born in 1652 and the Peter Künzi who purchased the lease in 1687. The name and place of origin match, but the remaining evidence is circumstantial.

Buchholterberg, in Switzerland, is a remote area east of the Aare River, north of Thun. Its isolation may have have made it relatively safe from the Anabaptist bounty hunters and the other persecutions of the Bernese government.

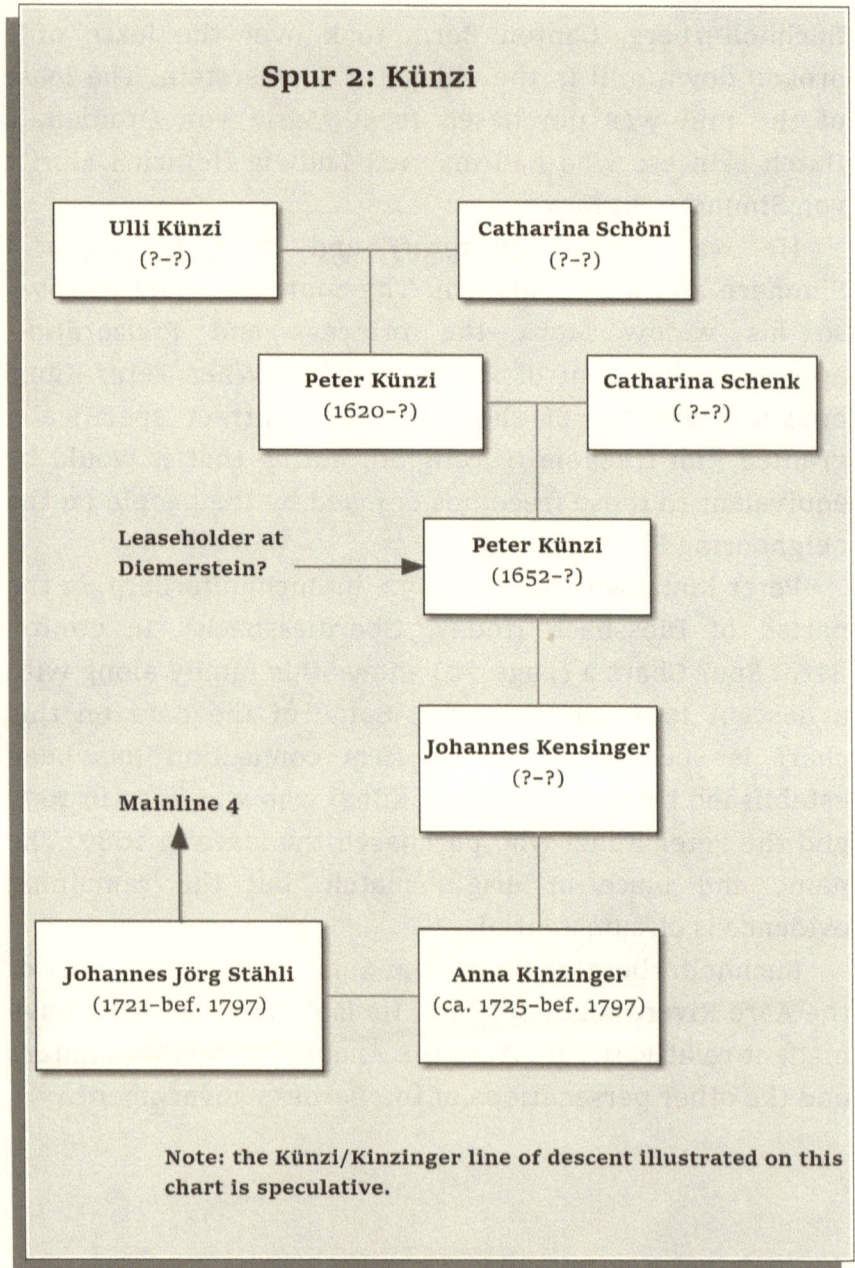

Spur 2: Künzi

Ulli Künzi
(?-?)

Catharina Schöni
(?-?)

Peter Künzi
(1620-?)

Catharina Schenk
(?-?)

Leaseholder at
Diemerstein? →

Peter Künzi
(1652-?)

Johannes Kensinger
(?-?)

Mainline 4

Johannes Jörg Stähli
(1721-bef. 1797)

Anna Kinzinger
(ca. 1725-bef. 1797)

Note: the Künzi/Kinzinger line of descent illustrated on this
chart is speculative.

One well-known Anabaptist family, that of Melchior Brennemann, was living there until the harsh measures of 1670/71, when he and his family went into exile in the Pfalz. Shortly thereafter, this family appeared on the Fischbacherhof, near Hochspeyer and Diemerstein. Doubtless this family, along with others, were the ones referred to at Fischbach when Peter Künzi was granted freedom of religion under the terms of the contract for lease of the mill.

When Peter Künzi sold the lease of the mill in 1698, one of the buyers was a son of Melchior Brennemann. Whether Peter Künzi and Melchior Brennemann were acquainted with each other in Buchholterberg is not known.

Much later, in the early years of the 19th century, Jacob Stähli, third son of Hans-Jörg Stähli and Anna Kinzinger, would marry, as his second wife, Elisabeth Brennemann, likely a relative of the Brennemann family on the Fischbacherhof, near Diemerstein.

At some point, members of the Künzi family began writing their name in the German fashion, adopting their surname as Kinzinger (or a similar surname—there were several variations).

A Mennonite census list from 1743 enumerates a Johannes Kensinger with his wife, two sons, and a daughter, living at Frankenstein (adjacent to Diemerstein).

It is possible that the daughter, not named in the census, is Anna Kinzinger, still living at home as an unmarried woman. If this Johannes Kensinger was the son (or grandson) of Peter Künzi, the Swiss immigrant who bought the lease of the mill in 1687, then this ties Anna

Kinzinger to him. This has not been proven, but it is a plausible scenario.

Anna Kinzinger and her husband Hans-Jörg Stähli were married sometime before the birth of their first child, Johannes, in 1750. Since Hans-Jörg was born in 1721, Anna Kinzinger was probably of a similar age, born circa 1725.

Diemerstein

Mennonites living at Diemerstein belonged to the Fischbach congregation, and later to the congregation at Sembach. Diemerstein is a very small hamlet consisting (today) of a single street of houses. It was probably even smaller in the early years of the 18th century. The village is in a narrow, dead-end valley. The surrounding hills are steep and thickly covered in woodland. There is a ruined castle overlooking the town, which feels isolated and remote.

A building that the Mennonites used for services was eventually erected near the mill. Some sources refer to this building as a small Mennonite church. It was demolished in the early part of the 19th century.

For many years in the 18th century, the Mennonites of Diemerstein were forbidden to bury their dead locally. They were obliged to carry their dead over a difficult forest path, in secret, to Fischbach. This path was known as the *Totenpfad*—the way of the dead. A Mennonite cemetery was built in Diemerstein in 1783.

Today, the busy main road to Hochspeyer and Kaiserslautern is nearby, along with the passenger railway. The train makes stops at the station in

Frankenstein, which is the administrative center for Diemerstein and the surrounding area.

Heinrich Stähli

Of the five (or six) children of Hans-Jörg Stähli, the fates of four of them are well-documented. First, I will discuss Heinrich Stähli, born 1751, and then provide a synopsis of the lives of his siblings in a spur chart. Heinrich's family is shown in Mainline Chart 5 (page 74).

For the period between the time of Heinrich Stähli's birth in 1751 in Diemerstein, and his first marriage in 1797, nothing is known. Of course, in his early years, he would have lived with his parents, either at Diemerstein or on one of the various farming estates where his father was employed. His father, Hans-Jörg Stähli, was a *Taglöhner*, a journeyman, who hired out for short-term work.

In 1797, Heinrich Stähli married Anna Widmer. His age was 46 years—rather old for a first marriage. It was recorded in the parish register of the Mennonite church at Sembach.

In June 1798, a daughter, Magdalena Stähli, was born. Anna Widmer died soon after, on the Hermersbergerhof, near Annweiler.

In 1829, Magdalena Stähli married Peter Latschar, who was born at Enkenbach in 1803. Latschar is a well-known Swiss-Mennonite surname. Magdalena Stähli died in 1841, leaving behind her husband and five children. The three youngest Latschar children emigrated to the United States.

Mainline 5: Heinrich Stähli

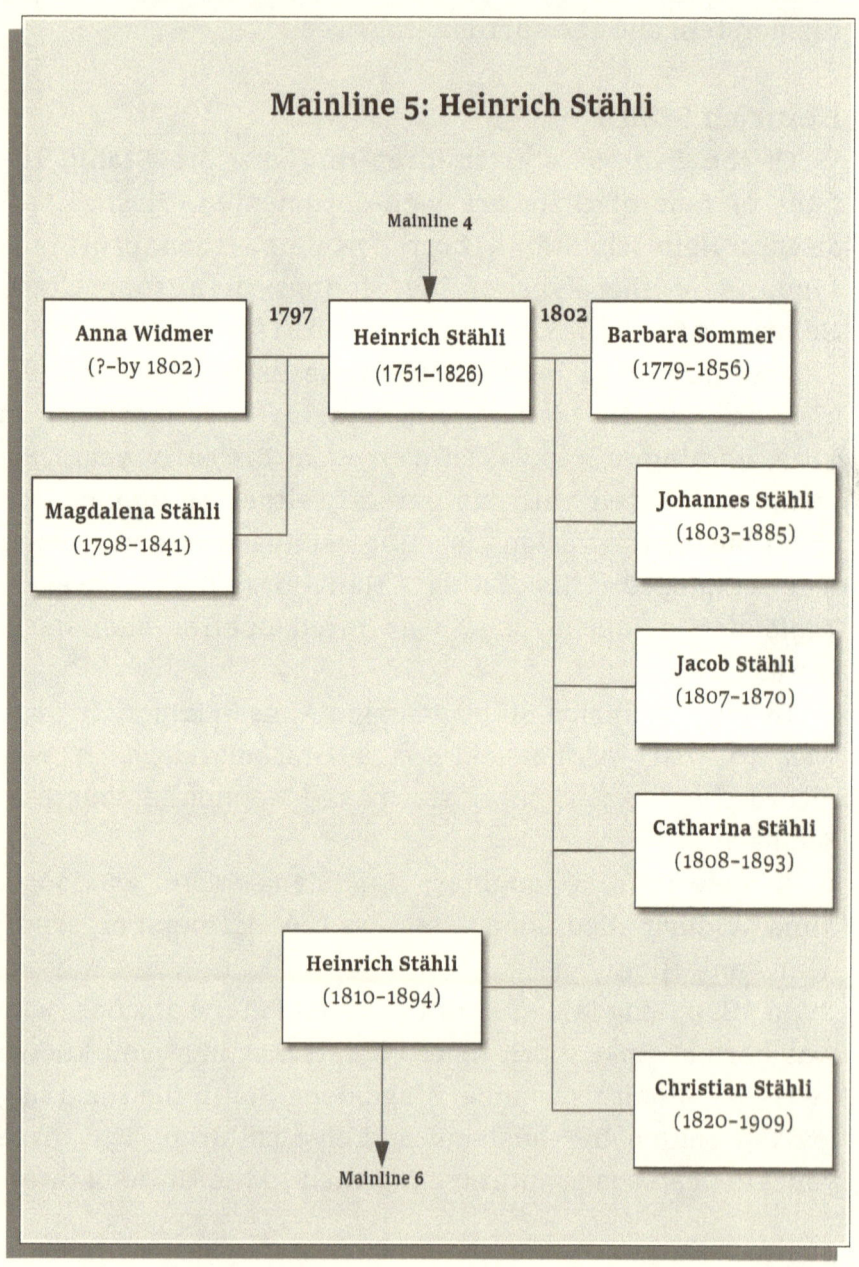

Mainline 4

| | 1797 | Heinrich Stähli (1751–1826) | 1802 | Barbara Sommer (1779–1856) |

Anna Widmer (?–by 1802)

Magdalena Stähli (1798–1841)

Johannes Stähli (1803–1885)

Jacob Stähli (1807–1870)

Catharina Stähli (1808–1893)

Heinrich Stähli (1810–1894)

Christian Stähli (1820–1909)

Mainline 6

Heinrich Stähli relocated to St. Germanshof, on the very southern edge of the German *Pfälzerwald*. There, in 1802, he married Barbara Sommer, born in 1779 on the Lindelbrunnerhof, an estate near Dahn. She was 28 years younger than her new husband. Barbara Sommer's parents were connected with St. Germanshof. Her mother, Anna Roggy, had been born there in about 1751, and her father, Joseph Sommer, had died there.

St. Germanshof is situated on the border between the German Pfalz and the French district of Alsace. Wissembourg, the nearest town, is in France.

Estates in area, such as St. Germanshof, had been associated with Amish-Mennonites for over 100 years. When the Anabaptist Caspar Joder family had left their home town of Steffisburg, in Canton Bern, in the 1690s, it relocated to the Langenberg estate, a neighbor of St. Germanshof. Johannes Joder, presumed son of Caspar Joder, was at St. Germanshof until about 1728.

St. Germanshof (2015)

A primary landowner in this area was Baron Ignace Louis Vitzthum von Egersberg. Nearby farming estates (for example, the Diefenbacherhof) around the Alsatian towns of Riedseltz and Wissembourg were mostly in the hands of Anabaptists, as leaseholders.

After French King Louis XIV proclaimed (in 1712) that Anabaptists in Alsace must leave, Baron Vitzthum intervened, and his Anabaptist tenants were allowed to remain, despite the protests of some local residents. Doubtless the economic benefits to Baron Vitzthum overrode the religious concerns of the French king and the local Catholic authorities.

The French civil authorities in the Alsatian hamlet of Weiler, very close to St. Germanshof,[6] registered the wedding of Heinrich Stähli and Barbara Sommer. The marriage document provides many interesting genealogical details, including the exact date of birth of Heinrich Stähli (June 30, 1751), place of birth (Diemerstein), that he was a widower, and that he was a farmer living at St. Germanshof.

Similar details were specified for the bride, Barbara Sommer, including that she had been living at Schleithal, an area in Alsace about 15 kilometers from St. Germanshof. The marriage date specified in the document is the "19th of Thermidor in the tenth year of the French Republic." This system of dates was instituted after the French Revolution and the founding of the French Republic in 1792. The date converts to August 7, 1802.

---

6 This border region has often passed between Germany and France. In 1802, France ruled the Pfalz, which was administered as the *Département de Monte Tonnerre*.

Witnesses at the wedding were Valentin Sommer, brother of the bride, and Johannes Suttor and Joseph Albrecht, both of whom were married to sisters of Heinrich Stähli, the groom.

While living at St. Germanshof, Heinrich Stähli and Barbara Sommer became the parents of four children: Johannes (1803), Jacob (1807), Catharina (1808), and Heinrich, the younger, in 1810. The records of the births of the three sons are in the archives of the French *département* of *Bas-Rhin*. The births were registered by French civil authorities in Weiler, the village closest to St. Germanshof. A gap in the records from the *Bas-Rhin* archives exists where the birth record of Catharina should be found. Her birth date has been derived from her 1893 obituary.

In addition to these four children, a fifth child, Christian, was born in 1820, probably in Diemerstein. At some point between the birth of Heinrich, the younger, in 1810, and Christian, in 1820, the family had moved back to their home in Diemerstein.

There, in 1826, Heinrich Stähli (the elder) died, as recorded by a local official at Frankenstein. The death record contains some inaccurate information, such as his age, and the name of his first wife. In addition to his widow, Barbara Sommer, he left behind their four sons and a daughter, and another daughter from his first marriage with Anna Widmer.

Sommer Family

I have discovered little about Barbara Sommer's heritage (Spur Chart 3, page 79). Her parents were Joseph Sommer and Anna Roggy, both of whom came from Swiss families with Amish-Mennonite traditions. On her maternal side, Anna's grandfather was Valentin Roggy, who had died on the Diefenbacherhof, in Riedseltz, Alsace.

Barbara Sommer's family was connected with St. Germanshof, as noted earlier, and with Schleithal, in Alsace, where Barbara and her brother had been living. It is possible that the Sommer and Roggy families had been living in or near Alsace since leaving Switzerland several generations earlier. In some records, the surname "Roggy" is written as "Rohée," which suggests a French influence.

After Joseph Sommer's death, his widow Anna Roggy married Christian Jutzi, who died near Wissembourg. Anna Roggy died in 1824, in Diemerstein, probably in the home of her daughter, Barbara Sommer.

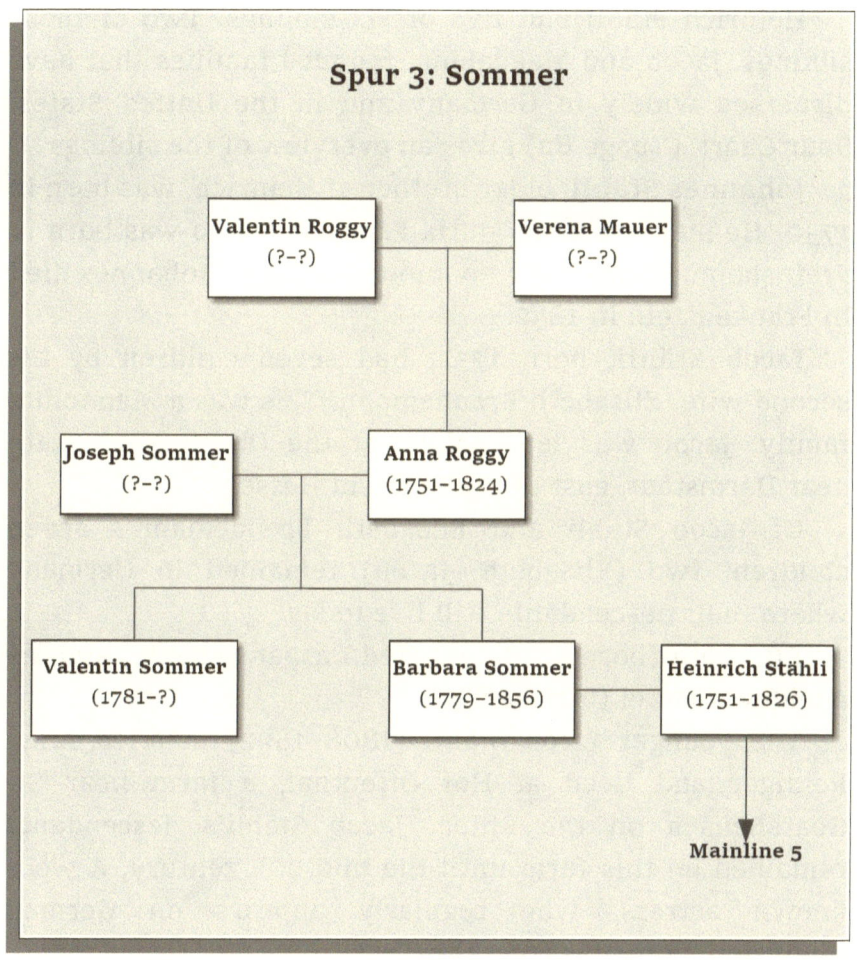

Spur 3: Sommer

Siblings

Heinrich Stähli had five or six siblings. Two of those siblings, Jacob and Magdalena, founded families that have dispersed widely in Germany and in the United States. Spur Chart 4 (page 82) gives an overview of the siblings.

Johannes Stähli, elder brother of Heinrich, was born in 1750. He married Anna Maria Friedauer, who was born in Freinsheim. There were no known children. Johannes died in Frankenstein in 1832.

Jacob Stähli, born 1752, had seven children by his second wife, Elisabeth Brennemann. This was a Mennonite family. Jacob was leaseholder at the Obertraysa estate near Darmstadt, east of the Rhine in Hesse.

Of Jacob Stähli and Elisabeth Brennemann's seven children, two (Elisabeth, Jacob) remained in Germany where their descendants still live today.

Elisabeth (born 1810) married Caspar Schantz, and, as a widow, Daniel Unzicker.

The younger Jacob Stähli (1808–1892) married Anna Reidiger and lived at Hof Offenthal, a farm near St. Goarshausen on the Rhine. Jacob Stähli's descendants remained on this farm until the mid 20th century. A well-known actress, who regularly appears on German television, descends from this line.

The elder Jacob Stähli's daughter, Katharina (born 1811), had died by the time her widowed mother gave up the lease of the Obertraysa estate in 1839. Katharina had married Friedrich Jutzi and had given birth to one daughter, Elise, born in 1836. In 1864, Elise Jutzi emigrated to Kansas along with her Jutzi half-siblings.

Friedrich Jutzi had married Helena Brennemann after the death of his first wife, and fathered seven additional children. He was the manager of a farming estate in Lüderbach, Hesse, where he died in 1851. His daughter, Elise, died in Coffey County, Kansas, in 1888.

The elder Jacob Stähli's four other children (Barbara, Magdalena, Peter, Christian) emigrated to the United States.

Barbara Stähli (born 1805) married Johann Christian Naffziger. They arrived in New York in 1853, and settled in Illinois.

Magdalena Stähli (born 1806) married Peter Erismann. Her brother, Peter Stähli (born 1813), married Catharina Güngerich. Both of these families emigrated on the ship *Janet Ridston* in 1852, and settled in Illinois and Nebraska.

Christian Stähli (born 1817), married Magdalena Unzicker. They were the parents of eleven children, many of whom did not survive into adulthood. The couple emigrated to the United States, where the family wrote their name "Staehly."

One of their sons, Robert, died in the Franco-Prussian War (1870-71). Another son, the younger Christian, emigrated to New York, where he was a brewer.

Descendants of these four families are numerous in Illinois, Wisconsin, Nebraska, and in many other locations.

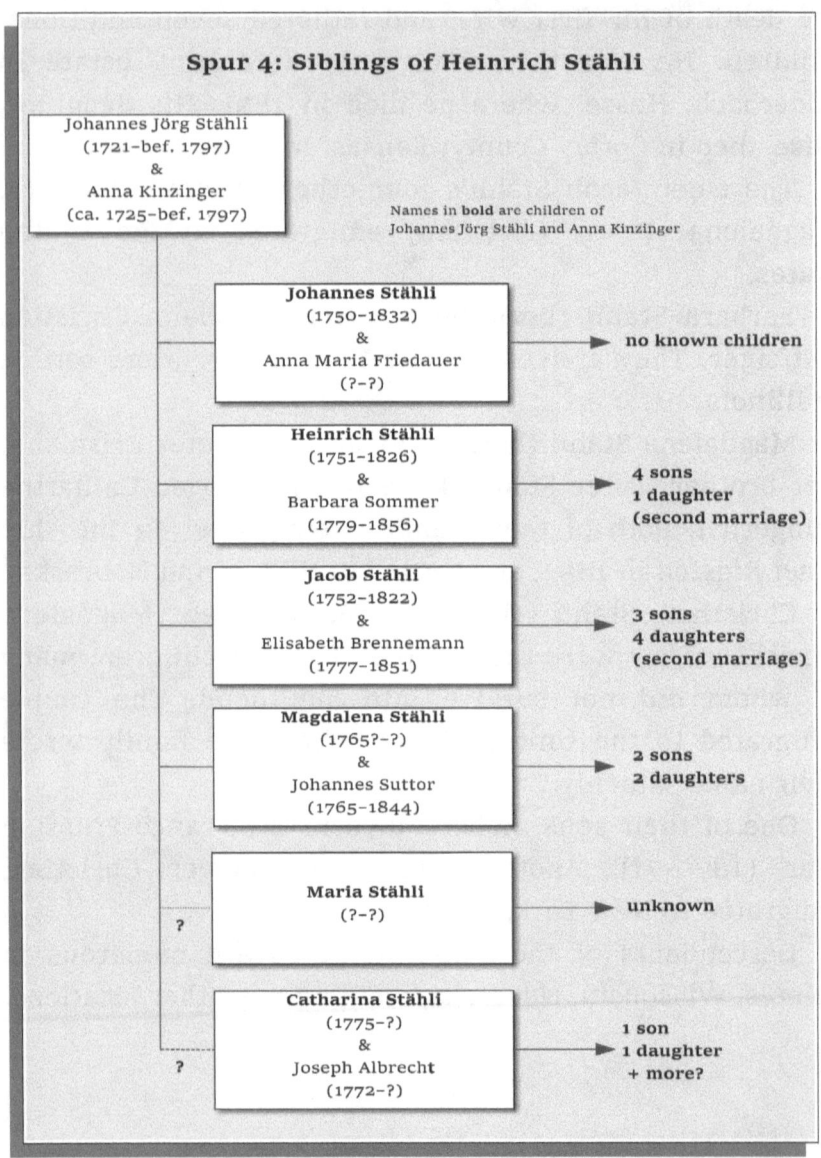

Spur 4: Siblings of Heinrich Stähli

Johannes Jörg Stähli
(1721–bef. 1797)
&
Anna Kinzinger
(ca. 1725–bef. 1797)

Names in **bold** are children of
Johannes Jörg Stähli and Anna Kinzinger

Johannes Stähli
(1750–1832)
&
Anna Maria Friedauer
(?–?)
→ no known children

Heinrich Stähli
(1751–1826)
&
Barbara Sommer
(1779–1856)
→ 4 sons
1 daughter
(second marriage)

Jacob Stähli
(1752–1822)
&
Elisabeth Brennemann
(1777–1851)
→ 3 sons
4 daughters
(second marriage)

Magdalena Stähli
(1765?–?)
&
Johannes Suttor
(1765–1844)
→ 2 sons
2 daughters

Maria Stähli
(?–?)
→ unknown

Catharina Stähli
(1775–?)
&
Joseph Albrecht
(1772–?)
→ 1 son
1 daughter
+ more?

Magdalena Stähli, sister to Heinrich Stähli, married Johannes Suttor, who was a witness at the 1802 wedding of Heinrich Stähli and Barbara Sommer. He was also a witness at the births of several of Heinrich and Barbara's children. There were four children (two sons, two daughters) in this Suttor family, which was Mennonite. Some branches emigrated to Bavaria and to the United States (where the name is written "Sutter"). There are numerous descendants on both sides of the ocean.

The details of the life of **Maria Stähli** are unknown. It is possible that she was the same person who was, as Catharina Stähli, living with her husband, Joseph Albrecht, at St. Germanshof. The German practice of employing the forename "Maria" for daughters suggests that Maria Stähli's full name was "Maria Catharina Stähli," and she used "Catharina" among family and friends.

At St. Germanshof in 1802, a child, Jacob Albrecht, was born to Joseph Albrecht and **Catharina Stähli**. Witnesses of the birth were Catharina's brother-in-law, Johannes Suttor, and her brother, Heinrich Stähli.

The parents' earlier child, Catharina Albrecht, was born in 1800. At that birth, the mother's age was noted as 25, computing to a birth year of 1775.

Joseph Albrecht and his family emigrated to Bavaria in about 1807. A document from the Bavarian archives indicates the family was Mennonite. Their son, Jacob (born 1802), may be the person denoted as a Mennonite in the 1871 census for the Huron district, Ontario, Canada.

It is likely these Albrechts were connected in some way to the Albrecht family that had lived at Hermersbergerhof, where Heinrich Stähli's first wife had died, and where Heinrich was probably working at the time of her death. Michael Albrecht had lived at Hermersbergerhof, where he was the leaseholder.

In 1802, Michael's grandson, Christian, married a woman from Diemerstein and emigrated to the United States. Christian's descendant, William Albrecht, married Alma Stahly, a sister of Roy Stahly (1893–1986).

3. Across the Ocean

The Emigrants

After the death of Heinrich Stähli, the elder, in 1826, his children started to transform their lives.

Magdalena Stähli, his daughter from his first marriage, wed Peter Latschar in 1829, as has been noted.

Catharina, a daughter from Heinrich's second marriage with Barbara Sommer, married Christian Egli in Frankenstein in 1830. Heinrich's eldest son Johannes emigrated to the United States in the early 1830s, married, and became the father of a daughter, born in 1834 in Ohio.

Also in 1834, Heinrich Stähli, the younger, was married.

The civil authorities at Frankenstein, in the district of Kaiserslautern, recorded the wedding on the 19th of July, 1834. The marriage document is witness to the political changes that had occurred in the Pfalz, as it indicates that Kaiserslautern was located in the kingdom of Bavaria. After the defeat of Napoleon in 1815, France relinquished possession of the Pfalz, which, under the terms of the peace treaties, had passed to Maximilian I, of Bavaria. By 1835, Ludwig I had become king.

The bride was Maria Magdalena Ehresmann, described as 24 years old and *"ledig,"* i.e., single (never married). Both of her parents were dead; her brother, Johannes Jacob Ehresmann (1806–1894), was the sole representative of her family at the wedding.

The groom was also described as *"ledig,"* and as a linen-weaver (*"Leinenweber"*), 24 years old, living at Diemerstein. The scribe who executed the marriage document wrote the groom's surname as "Stähly," in the German fashion, as did Heinrich himself, who signed the document. Heinrich Stähli's name was to be transformed even further.[1]

---

1   When the younger Heinrich Stähli emigrated to the United States in 1835, he began to transform himself from Heinrich Stähli into Henry Stahly. The passenger manifest from his emigrant ship shows his name as "Henry Staehli," deftly combining his Swiss surname with an anglicized first name. I will call him Heinrich Stähli, the younger, or Heinrich, the emigrant, until his arrival in New York, at which point he becomes "Henry Stahly" as far as this book is concerned.

In January 1835, the local authorities at Diemerstein registered the birth of a child, Johannes. The parents were named as Magdalena Ehresmann and Heinrich Stähli. This would prove to be incorrect. The mother of Johannes was, of course, Magdalena Ehresmann, Heinrich Stähli's wife, but subsequent events showed that the biological father of Johannes was not Heinrich. See the Ehresmann section, on page 97.

In the summer 1835, the entire extended family left Diemerstein and made their way to Le Havre, the seaport on the coast of France. How they traveled overland from Diemerstein to Le Havre is not known—by foot or by horse-drawn conveyance were the only possibilities. The route took them to Saarbrücken and Metz (where the local authorities stamped Heinrich's passport, which had been issued in Karlsruhe) and through northern France to the English Channel.

There, they embarked onto the *SS France*, bound for New York. The party consisted of Heinrich Stähli, his wife Magdalena, and the eight month old baby Johannes; Heinrich's mother, Barbara Sommer; and Heinrich's sister, Catharina, together with her husband, Christian Egli, and their young daughter, Barbara Egli. Two of Heinrich's brothers, Jacob and Christian, were also on board the ship.

The emigrant party consisted of nine people, including two young children. The only missing person from the family was eldest brother Johannes Stähli (born 1803).

The reason that the family decided to emigrate was most likely economic. Although there were opportunities in the Pfalz for obtaining the long-term lease of a farm, the possibilities for actual land ownership were limited. The allure of inexpensive farmland across the ocean would have been irresistible to people who faced a difficult life toiling on other peoples' land for the profit of the landowner.

Escape from religious persecution had become less of a factor by the mid 19th century. On the other hand, the choice of a large Amish-Mennonite community in Wayne County, Ohio, where the emigrants first resided, suggests that the presence of a sympathetic group of coreligionists was a contributing factor in the decision to emigrate.

Johannes Stähli, or John, as he became known, had emigrated several years before, preparing the way for his brothers, sister and mother. He likely had sent back reports from Ohio detailing the conditions there, and how the journey across the ocean should be made. Although a ship passenger manifest with his name has not been found, his eldest child, Catherine, was born in Ohio in 1834, so he had been in the United States at least a year before the rest of the family. The 1840 Federal Census for Green Township, Wayne County, lists "John Staley" along with a wife and three children. Although only the head-of-household was identified by name in the 1840 census, the number/age/gender of the people listed match the known family of John Stahly at that time.

The *France* arrived in New York on October 27, 1835. The journey across the ocean took many weeks, of course. The ship was wind-powered, since steamships were not yet usual on ocean voyages. The ship may have stopped in England for supplies and additional passengers, although no one from the British Isles is listed on the passenger manifest, which the ship's master, Edward Funk, from Le Havre, provided in New York.

The nation of origin of the first six of the emigrant party is stated as "France," while the remaining three emigrants' nation of origin is stated as "Bavaria"—an interesting inconsistency.

After landing in lower Manhattan, the family made its way to Ohio, where John Stahly was living.

According to a sketch of Christian Stahly (born 1820) in a biographical history of Elkhart County, Indiana, the family first went to Stark County, Ohio, for the winter. Later, they moved to Wayne County, the adjacent county to the west.

Wayne County was excellent farming country. By 1835, scores of Amish and Mennonite families had settled there. Mennonites from Switzerland had founded the Sonnenberg community in 1819. Amish-Mennonites from Lancaster, Somerset and Mifflin counties in Pennsylvania had also relocated to the area. The tendency of the Amish and Mennonites to have very large families had encouraged some families to move west looking for inexpensive farmland. Today, Wayne County has one of the largest populations of Amish-Mennonites in North America, along with Elkhart County, Indiana.

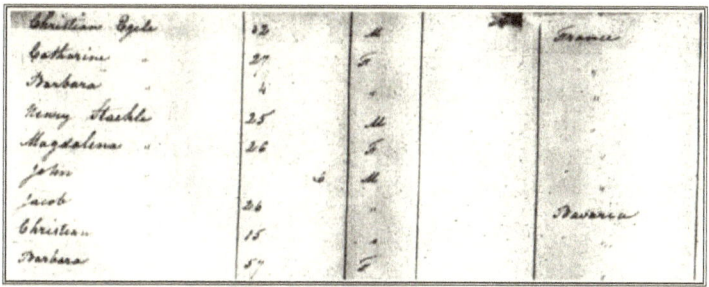

Passenger Manifest, extract, SS France at New York, 1835.
Credit: National Archives.

The 1840 Federal Census lists "Henry Staley" in Milton Township, north of Green Township, where Henry's brother John was living. The census shows many familiar Amish-Mennonite names in the immediate neighborhoods of the two brothers. The other brothers, Jacob and Christian, along with their mother Barbara Sommer, have not been located in the 1840 census, but they were probably nearby, as well. Catharine Stahly and her husband Christian Egli were in Holmes County, directly adjacent to Wayne County. Their daughter, Catharine Egli, was born there in 1837.

Before 1850, however, everyone in the Stahly emigrant families had relocated to Elkhart County, Indiana. Elkhart County had been opened for large-scale pioneer re-settlement in the early 1830s, after the original Native American population had been displaced. Settlers from Wayne County and other places made the trek westward. Many were Amish-Mennonites.

The 1850 Federal Census for Union Township, Elkhart County, enumerates brothers Jacob, Henry, and Christian Stahly in neighboring parcels. Their mother, Barbara Sommer, was living with her unmarried son, Jacob. John Stahly was nearby, in Locke Township. Christian Egli and his wife Catharine Stahly were further east in the county, in Clinton Township.

When these families made the move from Ohio is not precisely known. Christian Stahly, the youngest son, made the journey first, shortly after he was married, in Ohio, in February 1842, and before the birth of his first child, Peter, in late October 1842. The reason for the move was doubtless the opportunity for land ownership.

Henry Stahly followed at some point between the birth of his son, Henry, in 1845 in Ohio, and the birth of his next child, Peter, in Indiana in 1847. He may have moved westward at the same time as his brother, John, whose son Christian was born in Ohio in 1844, but whose daughter Lydia was born in Indiana in 1848.

Nappanee did not exist at that time. The area that became Elkhart County was originally known as the Elkhart Prairie. The name was taken from Shawnee Chief Elkhart, who was a cousin of Tecumseh and the father of the legendary maiden, Mishawaka.

The prairie had been populated by Native Americans, the Pottawatomi. Under treaties negotiated by the U.S. Government in the 1820s and early 1830s, the Pottawatomi lost their traditional lands, and were removed to Kansas. The area then began to be re-populated by newcomers, at first from New England, and later from Ohio and Pennsylvania.

Elkhart County was platted in 1830. Dunlap was its first county seat; Goshen, in the geographic center of the county, soon replaced it. The area in which the Stahly emigrants settled is located in the extreme southern part of the county, on the county line with Kosciusko County. The region was densely wooded, and some areas were swampy.

Travel from Ohio would have been via oxen or horse-driven carts over roads that were certainly very primitive, at best. When the emigrants arrived in Elkhart County, they would have had no shelter until they built it for themselves. The pioneers would have quickly cleared woodland and drained fields so that crops could be planted as soon as possible. This suggests an arrival in early spring, before planting season. Winters in northern Indiana can be cold and snowy. Shelter and adequate food stores were mandatory.

Despite these challenges, the emigrant families thrived. By 1860, 30 grandchildren had been born to Heinrich Stähli and Barbara Sommer (although neither grandparent was living: Barbara Sommer had died in 1856). Not all of the grandchildren survived to adulthood, but the ones that did formed the basis for a large, extended family in Elkhart County.

Henry Stahly

Mainline Chart 6 (page 93) illustrates the family of Henry Stahly (born "Heinrich Stähli" in 1810). By 1856, it consisted of his wife, Magdalena, their eight children, and John (formerly Johannes), born 1835, son of Magdalena Ehresmann.

Mainline 6: Heinrich Stähli, the emigrant

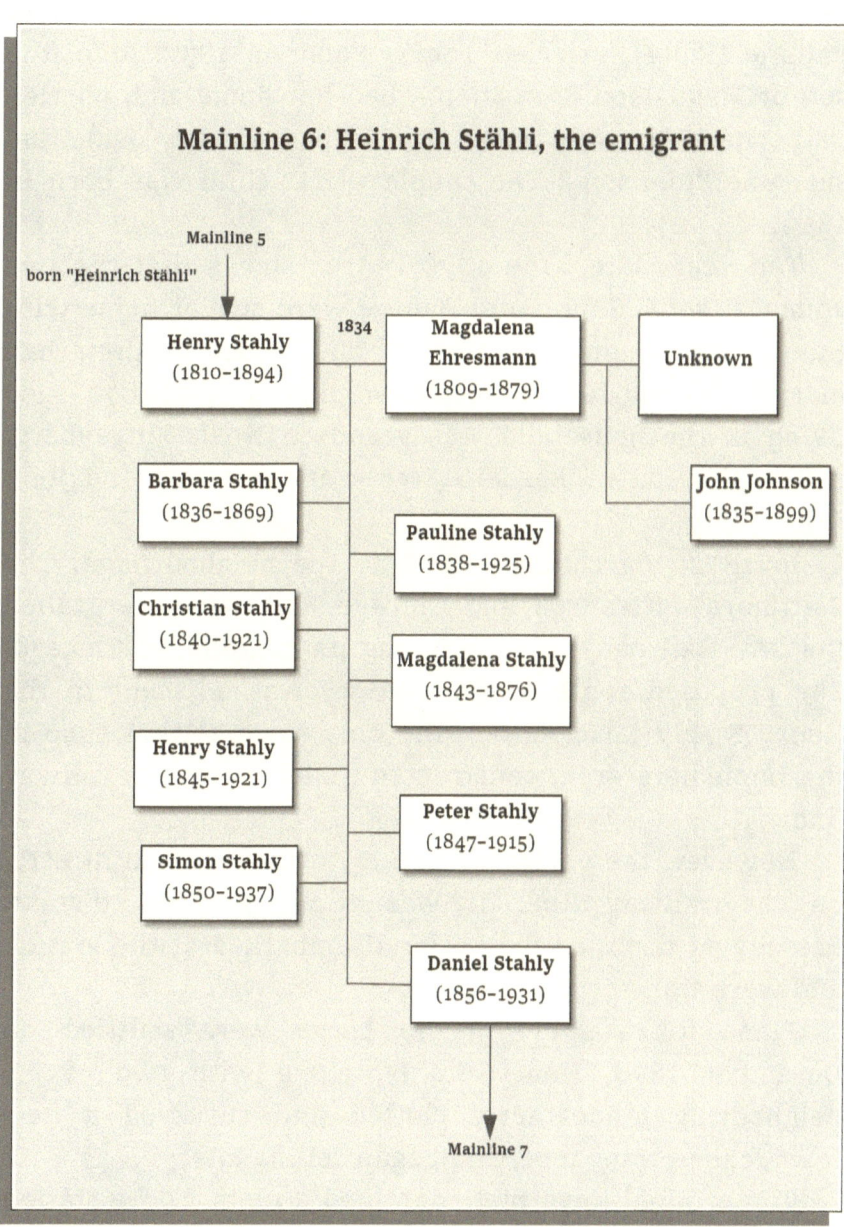

Mainline 5

born "Heinrich Stähli"

Henry Stahly
(1810–1894)

1834

Magdalena Ehresmann
(1809–1879)

Unknown

Barbara Stahly
(1836–1869)

Pauline Stahly
(1838–1925)

John Johnson
(1835–1899)

Christian Stahly
(1840–1921)

Magdalena Stahly
(1843–1876)

Henry Stahly
(1845–1921)

Peter Stahly
(1847–1915)

Simon Stahly
(1850–1937)

Daniel Stahly
(1856–1931)

Mainline 7

By 1860, those family members living at home had decreased. The eldest daughter, Barbara Stahly, had married John Ringenberg in 1853. The second eldest child, Pauline (Polly), married Tobias Yoder in 1857. John, the son of Magdalena Ehresmann, had left home and married Catherine Farmwald in 1858. He had started using the surname "Johnson." The couple's first child was born in 1859.

Ten years later, the 1870 census shows that the two youngest sons, Simon and Daniel, were still at home with Henry Stahly and Magdalena. The other children had married, except for Peter, who would marry in 1872. Also living in the household was grandson Noah Ringenberg, age 2, the son of Barbara Stahly and her husband John Ringenberg.

In 1872, big changes came to the neighborhood. The Baltimore, Pittsburgh and Chicago Railroad (later called the B&O Railroad) was extending its mainline to Chicago. The proposed route of the railway was adjacent to the Henry Stahly farm. Locke, the only town at that time in the immediate area, constructed a station on the railway line.

However, the village of Locke was not located directly on the railway line: it was about 3 miles distant. Passengers destined for Locke disembarked at the station and were transferred by horse.

Plans for a spur line to Locke were scuttled. In December 1874, Henry Stahly, along with two of his neighboring landowners, platted and surveyed a new town, called Nappanee, and began selling lots.

The original town plat contained 50 lots. Locke station was surrounded by the new village, which expanded very quickly. Nappanee—being directly on the mainline railway to Chicago—soon outpaced its neighbor, Locke. Today, Locke remains a hamlet; Nappanee is a town of about 6500 inhabitants. The name "Nappanee" is probably from Algonquian, a Native American language.

The 1870s also brought changes to the religious community in the new town of Nappanee. At first, the Amish-Mennonite congregation had been meeting in members' homes. Later, the congregation contributed funds for the construction of a schoolhouse, in 1867, which was then shared with the pupils.

Elkhart County had attracted many members of the Amish and Mennonite sects, especially from Wayne and Holmes counties, Ohio. One of these Mennonites, Isaac Smucker, had moved to Clinton Township, east of Goshen, in 1841. There, he was present at the first Amish service in Indiana, on Easter Sunday, 1842, and in 1843 he became the first Amish-Mennonite bishop in Indiana.

After the Old Order Amish broke off in the schisms of the early 1860s in Indiana,[2] Smucker remained with the more progressive, reform-minded branch, which usually referred to itself as the "Amish-Mennonite" church.

The small Amish-Mennonite congregation at Nappanee also remained in the progressive wing. Their pastor was John Ringenberg, who had come to the United States with his mother at about the same time as the Stahly emigrants,

---

2 Schisms have been frequent and painful occurrences in the history of the Amish and Mennonite denominations. The original schism, between Jacob Ammann and Hans Reist, resulted in the Amish/Mennonite split. Schisms were usually disagreements about theology, religious practices, matters of personal appearance (such as the length of an unmarried man's hair, or how fancy a woman's bonnet could be), or over which piece of modern technology was acceptable. Although these squabbles seem trivial, they resulted in bitter and often permanent divisions within the congregations.

and had relocated to Elkhart County along with them. In 1853, he married Henry Stahly's eldest child, Barbara, and they became the parents of six children. In February 1869, Barbara, who was pregnant, died after falling from a wagon. Her widower, John Ringenberg, died in 1871, leaving behind six orphaned children. Barbara Stahly and her husband John Ringenberg were both buried in what became known as the Union Center cemetery, a few miles north and east of Nappanee. Many other family members would be buried there, as well, when their time came.

The unexpected death of John Ringenberg left the Amish-Mennonite congregation at Nappanee without a pastor. This was remedied by the arrival in town of Jonathan Smucker, son of Isaac Smucker, the bishop. Jonathan himself also became a bishop.

In 1875, thirteen members of the Nappanee congregation formally organized a church, which became known as the West Market Street Mennonite Church, and, eventually, the First Mennonite Church of Nappanee. Henry Stahly and his wife, Magdalena; their son Christian Stahly and his wife; Magdalena (daughter of Henry and Magdalena); and John Johnson (Magdalena Ehresmann's son) and wife, were among the charter members. Seven of the thirteen charter members were Stahly family members. Jonathan Smucker was the pastor.

The first church building was constructed in 1878, exactly 200 years after the rebuilding of the church in Sigriswil, where Caspar Stähli was baptized.

The years 1870–1880 were pivotal for Henry Stahly and Magdalena Ehresmann. Henry had sold his original homestead and moved to the farm in Locke Township that had been owned by his late son-in-law, John Ringenberg, and his daughter Barbara. Nine of Henry and Magdalena's grandchildren had been orphaned, and Magdalena herself died in 1879, following a short illness, according to her obituary.

Ehresmann

Magdalena Ehresmann's ancestors can be traced back to Christian Ehresmann, who represented the Essingen congregation at the 1779 conference of Amish elders (also at Essingen), when the Amish Discipline was adopted. Although the surname is Swiss, I have not been able to trace the exact place of origin for the family. Spur Chart 5 (page 98) shows the Ehresmann heritage.

Maria Magdalena Ehresmann was born in Pfiffligheim, near Worms, along the Rhine, in 1809. She was the daughter of *Taglöhner* Johannes Jacob Ehresmann (ca. 1785–bef. 1834) and Anna Barbara Fischer. Her birth was registered in French by the civil authorities.

Magdalena's two brothers emigrated to the United States, and became neighbors with each other in Clinton County, in central Indiana. Johannes Jacob, who had been a witness at his sister's marriage in 1834, married Katharina Ehresmann, his second cousin. His brother, Johannes Ehresmann, married Katharina Ehresmann's sister, Veronica, called Fanny.

Whether the three Ehresmann siblings in Indiana ever visited each other is not known. Nappanee and Clinton County are approximately 100 miles apart.

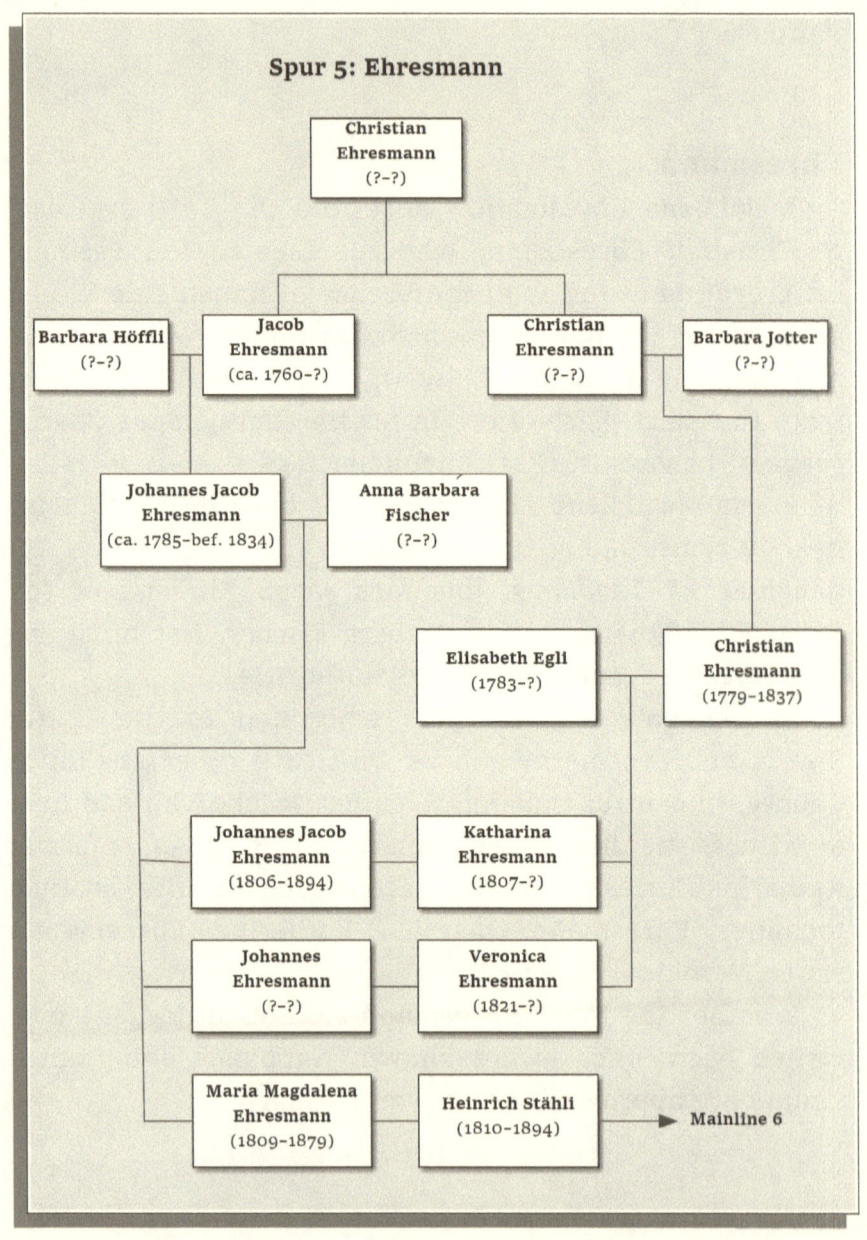

Spur 5: Ehresmann

There is a family legend about a traveling salesman who had visited both Magdalena Ehresmann and one of the Ehresmann households in Clinton County, and who is said to have made the connection between the siblings.

When Magdalena and Heinrich Stähli were married, in July 1834, she was carrying another man's child. The father of the child (who later used the name John Johnson, born in 1835) is not known.

For whatever reason, the father would not, or could not, marry Magdalena. Perhaps he was already married, had disappeared, had died, or was unwilling to marry.

Some have speculated that Magdalena Ehresmann had been married before her marriage with Heinrich Stähli, and had been left a widow. This is possible, of course, although the marriage document is explicit in designating her as "*ledig*," i.e., single, never married.

I do not find it likely that the surname "Johnson" proves that the father of the child was named "Johnson"—that is not a surname that was used in Germany. Perhaps the surname was employed in the United States to indicate that the child, John, was the son of John, and thus the surname became "Johnson," i.e., John's son, in the Scandinavian manner. Alternatively, it may have been a random choice to use the surname "Johnson."

When Henry Stahly, Magdalena's widower, died in 1894, his will referred to John Johnson as "his wife's son," and he was left a half-share of the estate, compared to the whole share each of the other heirs received.

John Johnson died in 1899 when he broke his neck after tumbling from a load of hay. His wife, Catherine Farmwald, had died a year earlier. They were survived by their four sons.

*

By 1890, all of Henry Stahly and Magdalena's children had married and had children of their own. Two of their children, Barbara and Magdalena, had died. There were six survivors, five sons and a daughter. When Henry Stahly died in 1894, only his younger brother, Christian (born 1820), of the emigrant generation, was still living.

Emigrant stories are often filled with difficult scenes of parting, when one family member departs, knowing that most likely he or she would never see left-behind parents or siblings again. Henry did not have this problem: he took his entire extended family with him across the ocean. The only family members he left behind in Europe in 1835 were his half-sister, Magdalena (who died in 1841), and numerous cousins, many of whom would themselves emigrate in the early 1850s.

Henry Stahly died on December 14, 1894, most likely at his farm in Locke Township. It was a long way in time (84 years) and space (4300 miles) from the farm on the Alsatian border where he had been born in 1810.

Henry Stahly's obituary appeared in the January 1895 issue of *Herald of Truth*, the weekly Mennonite magazine.

The brick church mentioned in the obituary was the Union Center Church of the Brethren, across the road from the cemetery. This building will make several additional appearances in this history.

Henry's stone is in the northeast corner of the cemetery, in the older section. His wife, Magdalena, is also buried there, as well as his two older brothers, John and Jacob, and his daughter, Barbara.

---

*STAHLY. Near Nappanee, Ind., of dropsy, **Henry Stahly**, died Dec. 14, 1894, aged 84 years, 10 months. He was united in marriage to Magdelena Erisman in 1834, lived in matrimony 45 years. His wife preceded him to the spirit world 15 years ago, the first of this month. He was born in Kaisers Lautern [sic] Germany, Feb. 1810. Emigrated to America in 1835 and settled in Wayne Co., Ohio; came to Elkhart Co., Ind. in 1846. He has resided here 48 years, has seen his children and grandchildren grow to manhood and womanhood, and the dense forest that once covered this beautiful country fall before the pioneer's axe. He was a consistent brother in the Amish Mennonite denomination, and while we pay the last tribute to him we realize that his seat will be vacant in church and at home. The surviving members are one brother, five sons, one daughter, 36 grandchildren and 12 great grandchildren. Buried at the Brick church on the 16th. Funeral services by Jas. H. McGowen in English and David Burkholder in German, from Job. 14: 14.*

NB: Henry Stahly was not born at Kaiserslautern, Germany. He was born at St. Germanshof, which at that time (1810) was part of France.

Emigrant Families

The histories of the emigrant families (siblings to Henry Stahly) have been lightly touched on, but I can add a few more details. A large number of people descend from the emigrant families. I am including brief, and by no means comprehensive, histories.

Spur Chart 6 (page 103) illustrates the emigrant siblings, their marriage partners, and their offspring.

Henry Stahly's stone at Union Center Cemetery

Spur 6: Siblings of Heinrich Stähli, the emigrant

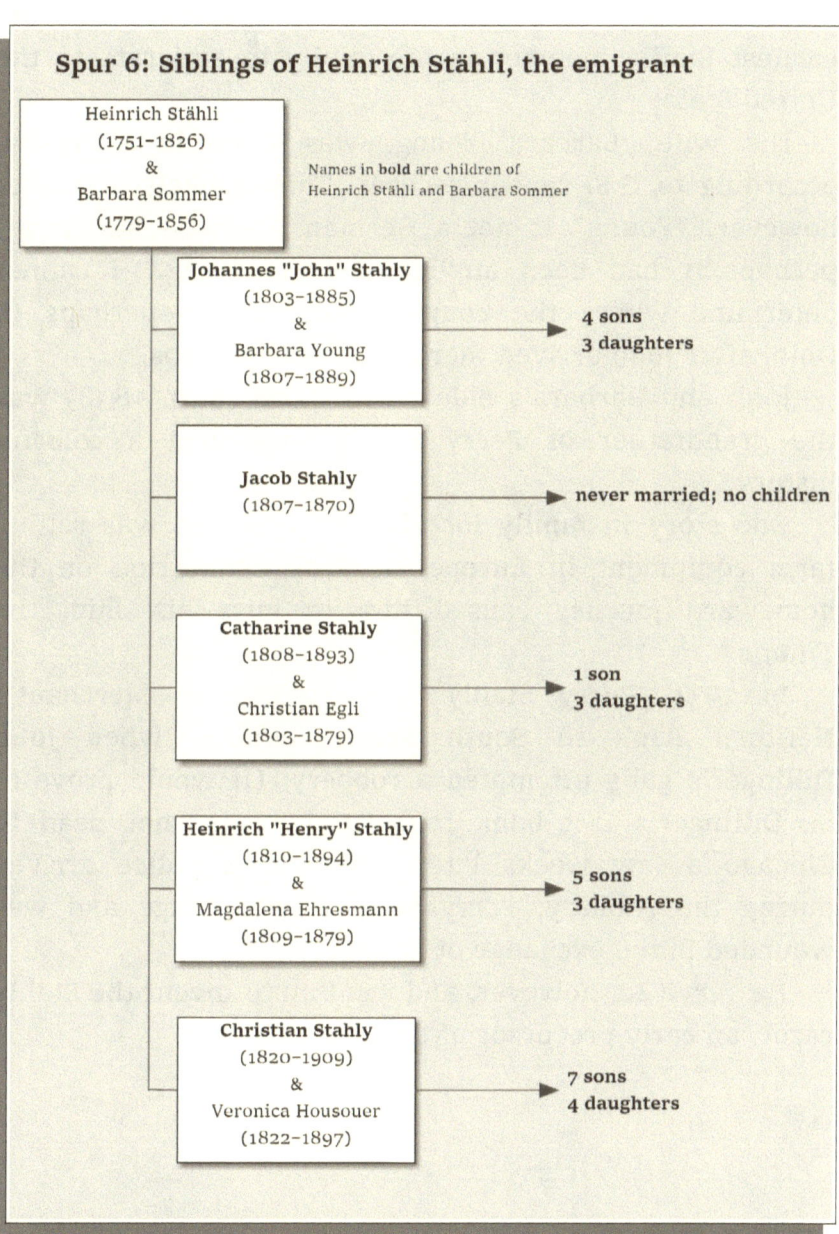

Heinrich Stähli
(1751-1826)
&
Barbara Sommer
(1779-1856)

Names in **bold** are children of
Heinrich Stähli and Barbara Sommer

Johannes "John" Stahly
(1803-1885)
&
Barbara Young
(1807-1889)

4 sons
3 daughters

Jacob Stahly
(1807-1870)

never married; no children

Catharine Stahly
(1808-1893)
&
Christian Egli
(1803-1879)

1 son
3 daughters

Heinrich "Henry" Stahly
(1810-1894)
&
Magdalena Ehresmann
(1809-1879)

5 sons
3 daughters

Christian Stahly
(1820-1909)
&
Veronica Housouer
(1822-1897)

7 sons
4 daughters

The children of emigrants **Henry Stahly** and Magdalena Ehresmann are discussed in the next chapter.

John Stahly (1803–1885), as noted earlier, was the earliest family member in his family to emigrate to the United States.

His wife, Barbara Young, was born in Germany, according to U.S. census records. This is likely accurate; however, "Young" is not a German or Swiss surname—perhaps it had been anglicized from "Jung." I cannot determine where the couple was married—perhaps in Ohio, after John arrived there in the early 1830s.

John and Barbara's eldest son Jacob (born 1838) was the grandfather of Perry Stahly, who had a colorful history.

One story in family lore is that when he was selling farm equipment in Europe, a tardy connection on the homeward journey caused him to miss his ship, the *Titanic*.[3]

In 1934, Perry Stahly was working at Merchant's National Bank in South Bend, Indiana, when John Dillinger's gang attempted a robbery. (It would prove to be Dillinger's last bank robbery: he was shot dead in Chicago a few weeks later.) When the police arrived during the robbery, Perry was taken hostage and was wounded in the exchange of gunfire.

He survived, however, and went on to invent the Stahly razor, an early precursor of the electric razor.

---

3 It is surprising how many family histories contain a *Titanic* story.

John Stahly's next youngest son, also named John (born 1842), was drafted into the Union army in 1863, and died during the American Civil War.

When John Stahly (the elder) died in 1885, his obituary noted that he had been blind for 20 or 30 years.

Emigrant **Jacob Stahly** (born 1807), never married. His mother, Barbara Sommer, kept house for him until she died in 1856. In the 1860 census, Jacob was living by himself on his farm in Union Township. By 1870, shortly before his death, he was living in the household of his younger brother, Christian.

Catharine Stahly (born 1808) and her husband Christian Egli lived on a farm in Clinton Township, east of Goshen. In 1879, Christian Egli died after a fall from a train while on a trip to visit a granddaughter in Miami County, Indiana. Catharine herself died in 1893, one year before her younger brother, Henry.

Christian Stahly (born 1820) was the only member of the emigrant generation to survive into the 20th century. Most of Christian and Fanny Stahly's children survived to marry and have children of their own. Their eldest son, Peter (1842-1924), relocated to Arkansas. Another son, Moses (1849-1926), moved to Kansas in 1893.

In Nappanee, the former farmhouse of Moses Stahly is listed on the National Register of Historic Places.

Christian Stahly died in 1909. Many interesting details about his 1842 journey from Ohio and his early days on the prairie were included in his obituary, which appeared in the *Gospel Herald:*

Stahley.- Christian Stahley was born in Germany, July 27, 1820; died in Nappanee, Ind., July 11, 1909; aged 88 y. 11 m. 14 d. The cause of his death was old age. He came to America with his mother, 3 brothers and 1 sister in 1835, and settled in Wayne Co.,O. Feb. 3, 1842, he was married to Fanny Housour, moved to Elkhart Co., Ind., the same year in a covered wagon drawn by an ox team. They had to live in this covered wagon for six weeks until the log cabin was completed. At that time wolves and deer were roaming through the dense forest, and many the hardships which they endured. He lived with his wife over 54 years, and to this union were born 11 children, 4 of whom died. He is survived by seven children, and a number of grandchildren and 2 great-grandchildren.

4. On the Elkhart Prairie

Daniel Stahly

On January 1, 1880, Daniel, the youngest son of Henry Stahly and his wife Magdalena, married Sarah Smucker in the home of the Rev. John Anglemeyer. Sarah Smucker was the daughter of Jonathan Smucker, the pastor at the newly established Amish-Mennonite church on the west side of Nappanee. She was born in 1859, in Wayne County, Ohio, and had moved around Ohio and Indiana with her father as he sought out inexpensive farmland and tended to church business.

There were several peculiar circumstances in the wedding of Daniel Stahly and Sarah Smucker.

Traditionally, the bride was married in her family home. In addition, weddings in Amish-Mennonite congregations were typically performed by a bishop. In this case, Sarah's father was a bishop, so it would have been usual for him to have performed the ceremony in his own home.

However, Jonathan Smucker had left for Illinois and Iowa, on church business, a few days before the planned wedding, of which he must have been aware. The wedding was conducted by John Anglemeyer at his house. Anglemeyer was pastor at the "brick church," i.e., the Union Center Church of the Brethren.

These circumstances could be explained by the fact that Daniel Stahly had not joined the Amish-Mennonite church,[1] and thus the marriage could not be officially blessed, especially if the bride's father was a bishop. Daniel Stahly was 23 years old at the time of his marriage, slightly older than usual, perhaps, for a young man from an Amish-Mennonite family not to have joined the church. He may have had doubts, or he may have simply put off taking the necessary steps.

It is likely that Jonathan Smucker did not approve of his daughter marrying someone not yet baptized into the Amish-Mennonite church. If he had refused to officiate at other weddings where both parties were not baptized

---

1 In the Amish and Mennonite denominations, adults explicitly decide to join the church, at which point he or she is baptized. Baptized persons are expected to remain faithful to the church; failure to do so is considered a serious offense.

members of the Amish-Mennonite church, he could hardly condone his daughter marrying a man not yet baptized.

Nevertheless, Sarah went forward with the wedding, either in opposition to her father's wishes or, more likely, with his tacit approval.

Why the Rev. Anglemeyer was chosen to perform the ceremony is not known. His denomination, the Church of the Brethren, was separate from the Amish-Mennonite denomination, although the similarities in the beliefs and practices between the two churches did create a very close alliance. Apparently, Rev. Anglemeyer was less exacting about the religious status of the young couple. Perhaps Anglemeyer was clairvoyant, and he saw that his granddaughter, Ethel Frederick, would marry, in 1916, Roy Stahly, Daniel and Sarah's fifth child.

Daniel Stahly was eventually baptized into the Amish-Mennonite church in 1881.

After the wedding, the couple moved in with Daniel's widowed father, Henry, who was living on the family farm north of Nappanee. The 1880 census shows that the Stahly household consisted of Daniel, Sarah, Henry (Daniel's father), and the orphaned Noah Ringenberg, Daniel's nephew.

Noah Ringenberg's elder brother, Henry Ringenberg, had married Mary Anne Smucker, younger sister of Sarah Smucker, in 1879.

Catherine Ringenberg, another of the orphans, married Rufus Smucker, Sarah and Mary Anne's brother, in 1886.

The mother of these Ringenberg orphans was Barbara Stahly, Daniel Stahly's sister. Interconnections such as these among the Stahly, Smucker, and Ringenberg families were not at all unusual among the Amish-Mennonite communities.

Harvey Stahly, Daniel and Sarah Stahly's first child, was born in 1883, and a daughter, Alma, followed in 1886.

Sarah Smucker and Daniel Stahly,
with Harvey and Alma, circa 1887

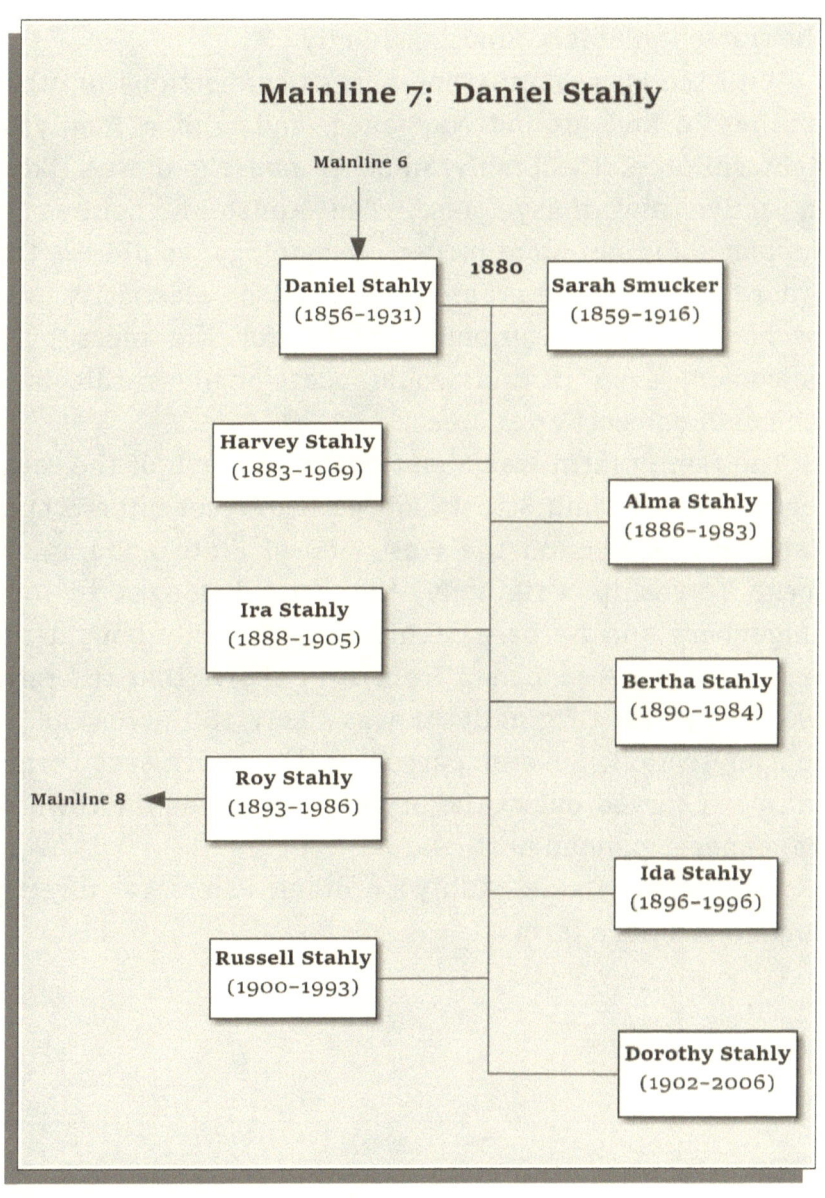

Mainline 7: Daniel Stahly

Mainline 6

Daniel Stahly
(1856–1931)

1880

Sarah Smucker
(1859–1916)

Harvey Stahly
(1883–1969)

Alma Stahly
(1886–1983)

Ira Stahly
(1888–1905)

Bertha Stahly
(1890–1984)

Mainline 8 ◄ Roy Stahly
(1893–1986)

Ida Stahly
(1896–1996)

Russell Stahly
(1900–1993)

Dorothy Stahly
(1902–2006)

Six more children were born to Daniel and Sarah: Ira (1888), Bertha (1890), Roy (1893), Ida (1896), Russell (1900), and Dorothy (1902). Mainline Chart 7 (page 111) illustrates the Stahly-Smucker family.

With the close family and church connections to other families in and around Nappanee, and with a family of eight children, the Stahly/Smucker household was likely an active and noisy place. The Amish-Mennonites at Nappanee did not shun modern technology, as did the Old Order Amish. Photography, telephones, electricity and mechanized farm equipment were, for the most part, welcomed, even if this would occasionally result in a schism of one sort or another.

The family farm was about one mile north of the town center (where Main Street and Market Street intersect) of Nappanee. It was on the west side of State Road 19, in Locke Township. Originally, this farm belonged to John Ringenberg and Barbara Stahly. Henry Stahly bought the farm in 1874. A plat map from 1915 shows that the farm was 134 acres. Originally, it was likely 160 acres, i.e., a quarter-section. Several parcels in the south-east corner had been carved out of the original parcel, as the town of Nappanee expanded northwards.

The farm of Daniel Stahly's brother, Peter, was directly north of Daniel's farm.

After Henry Stahly died in 1894, his son Daniel bought the Locke Township farm from the other heirs—presumably, Daniel's brothers (Christian, Henry, Peter, Simon), and his sister, Polly. Daniel's half-brother John Johnson could also have been an heir.

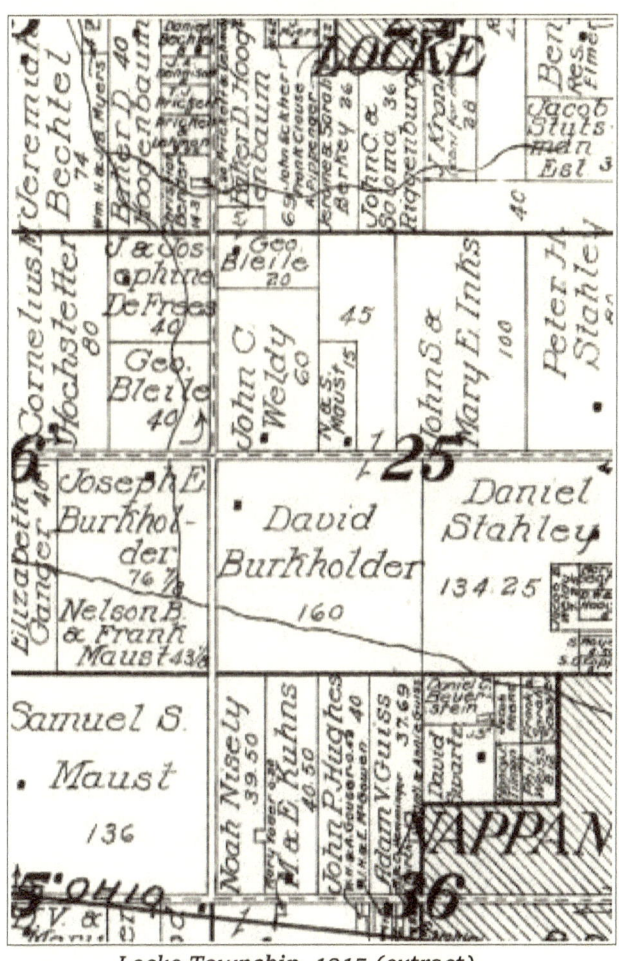

Locke Township, 1915 (extract)

Nappanee has since grown up around the farm, but in those days it was in the countryside. Farm buildings are still standing at the site. Although the house appears to have been extensively remodeled, the barn is likely much as it appeared when Daniel and Sarah lived there over a hundred years ago.

At one time, Henry Stahly, Daniel's father, had farmed east of Main Street, in Union Township. Those acres had been sold off as small parcels when the town of Nappanee was founded. It is not known how profitable Henry Stahly's land-selling business had been in 1874. The original land had likely been homesteaded, with very little or no cash outlay.

Stahly Farm in Locke Township, Nappanee (2016)

All five sons of Henry Stahly became substantial landowners, with farms in Locke and Union Townships in 1915, so it is possible that the sons were the ultimate beneficiaries of the sale of lots to create the town of Nappanee.

Smucker

Sarah Smucker was born in 1859.[2] She was the second child of Jonathan Smucker and Salome Peight. Eleven children were born to the couple. Two died young.

Spur Chart 7 (page 116) shows the Schmucker/Smucker family.

In 1856, Jonathan Smucker (1834–1903) married Salome Peight (1837–1893), daughter of Christian Peight and Sarah Zook. Peight family tradition claims that Christian Peight's mother was of Shawnee heritage.

---

2   As was the case with many surnames, "Smucker" had been transformed on its journey from Switzerland. The original Swiss spelling was "Schmocker," which became "Schmucker" and then "Smoker" in some branches of the family. Isaac Smucker and his son, Jonathan, felt that Amish-Mennonites should not be "Smokers"—they began to write their name as "Smucker."

Spur 7: Smucker

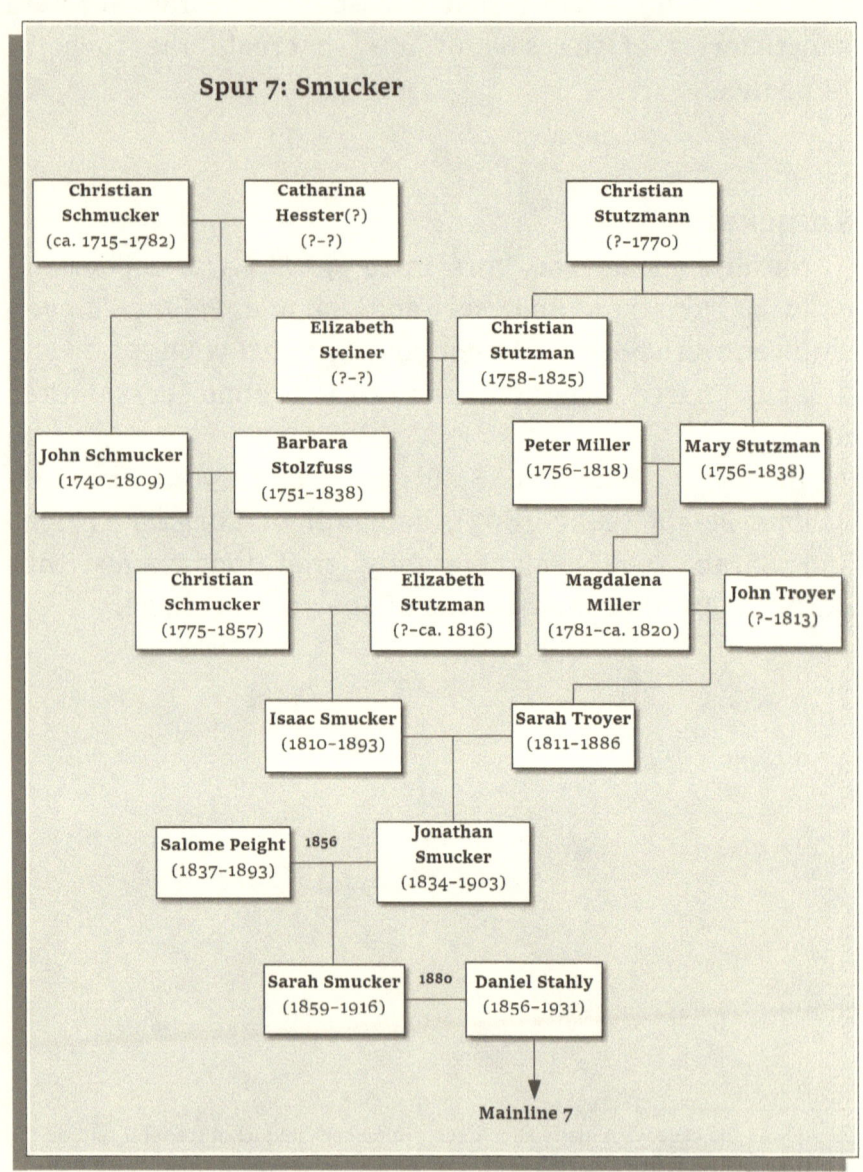

Christian Schmucker (ca. 1715–1782) — Catharina Hesster(?) (?–?)

Christian Stutzmann (?–1770)

Elizabeth Steiner (?–?) — Christian Stutzman (1758–1825)

John Schmucker (1740–1809) — Barbara Stolzfuss (1751–1838)

Peter Miller (1756–1818) — Mary Stutzman (1756–1838)

Christian Schmucker (1775–1857) — Elizabeth Stutzman (?–ca. 1816)

Magdalena Miller (1781–ca. 1820) — John Troyer (?–1813)

Isaac Smucker (1810–1893) — Sarah Troyer (1811–1886

Salome Peight (1837–1893) — 1856 — Jonathan Smucker (1834–1903)

Sarah Smucker (1859–1916) — 1880 — Daniel Stahly (1856–1931)

Mainline 7

Sarah Smucker's paternal ancestor was from a clan which had been among the early Amish-Mennonite families to come to Lancaster County. Her great-great-great-grandfather, Christian Schmucker, who died in 1782, had been born (probably) in the Swiss village of Grindelwald in about 1715.[3] Grindelwald is located directly under the craggy peak of the Eiger, one of the most famous mountains in the Swiss Alps. It is fitting that the Eiger is one of the many peaks that can be seen from Sigriswil, many kilometers away on the *Thunersee*.

At some point, Christian Schmucker became an Anabaptist. In 1745, he was imprisoned for four days at Trachselwald, a fortress/prison in the Emmental.

The record of payment to the bailiff (who escorted Christian Schmucker to Trachselwald) indicates that the prisoner was a *"Pietistenlehrer aus dem Grindelwald"* i.e., a pietistic teacher, from Grindelwald.

Christian went into exile at Montbéliard, today in France, but at that time belonging to the duke of Württemberg, who had a tolerant attitude about religious non-conformists. When the French king had expelled Anabaptists from Alsace in 1712, Montbéliard became a place of refuge.

Christian had married Catharina Hesster (or Hässler) and had fathered four children. In 1752, a passport was issued at Montbéliard to Christian Schmucker and his family.

---

3   It is possible that Christian Schmucker was born elsewhere, as there were several Schmocker families in Canton Bern. One of these families was in Beatenberg, on the north shore of the *Thunersee*, the next parish over from Sigriswil.

They traveled down the Rhine to Rotterdam, across the ocean on the ship *St. Andrew*, to Philadelphia, arriving in September 1752.

A large tract of land—Pennsylvania—had been granted by the English King, Charles II, to William Penn, who had welcomed religious non-conformists. Lancaster County was a favored destination for many Amish-Mennonite immigrants.

After the American Revolution started in 1776, family legend has it that Christian Schmucker was imprisoned for refusing to join the Pennsylvania militia. When Christian arrived in Philadelphia in 1752, he had signed an oath of allegiance to the English king. It may have been this oath that was the reason for Christian's refusal to join the revolutionary militia, or it may have been the pacifism of his Mennonite beliefs.

Trachselwald. ☺ *Jakob Samuel Weibel (1771–1846).*
(Swiss National Library)

In either case, it seems that his age should have excused him from duty.

As more immigrants arrived in Pennsylvania, some families moved west in search of cheaper land. Christian Schmucker's grandson, also named Christian (1775–1857), moved to Wayne County, Ohio, sometime after the death of his first wife, Elizabeth Stutzman. Christian Schmucker and Elizabeth Stutzman had ten children. Christian and his second wife, Fanny Livengood, had an additional eight. Christian Schmucker and Elizabeth Stutzman's son, Isaac (1810–1893), moved further west, to Elkhart County, Indiana.

When Isaac Smucker married Sarah Troyer in 1832, his new wife was also his second cousin. Both Isaac Smucker and Sarah Troyer could trace their heritage to Christian Stutzmann and Barbara Hochstetler. Isaac was descended from Christian Stutzman (the younger, born 1758); Sarah Troyer was descended from Christian Stutzman's sister, Mary Stutzman, who was born in 1756.

Due to the relatively early arrival of the Schmucker family in Lancaster County, and the tendency of the Amish-Mennonites to choose marriage partners from within their own community, such relationships were not uncommon.

Ancestors of Sarah Smucker include those from some of the oldest and best-known surnames among the Amish-Mennonites in Pennsylvania, including Yoder, Stutzman, Stoltzfus, Miller, Zook, Hochstetler and Troyer. Chapter 5 (page 145) provides more details on this topic.

Jonathan Smucker Family, 1887. Back row, from left: Menno (pasted in), John, Rufus, Milo. Middle: Ida, Mary Anne, Jonathan, Salome (née Peight), Sarah. Front: Frank, Jesse.

Sarah Smucker (1859–1916) was second cousin to Jerome M. Smucker, who founded the J.M Smucker Company in Wooster, Ohio, and whose name is almost synonymous with jams and jellies. Jerome Smucker was the grandson of David Smucker (born 1805), who was Isaac Smucker's elder brother.

Sarah Smucker's mother Salome died in 1893, and her father Jonathan died ten years later. Both are buried in the cemetery at Union Center. When Sarah died in 1916, seven of her eight children were still living. Ira Stahly, third child of Daniel and Sarah, had died from heart problems in 1905. Her youngest child, Dorothy, was 14 years old. Several of Sarah's children had married, and she had four grandchildren. Sarah was also survived by five brothers and two sisters.

Nappanee Siblings

Daniel Stahly and Sarah, along with his siblings and their spouses, produced a large number of cousins, most of whom remained in the Nappanee area. Magdalena Ringenberg, the daughter of Barbara Stahly and John Ringenberg, was the eldest of the cousins, born in 1856. The youngest cousin was Dorothy Stahly, born in 1902. She was the daughter of Daniel Stahly and Sarah Smucker.

The large age difference among the Stahly cousins likely placed them in different social circles. This age spread was the result of the 20 year difference between the age of the eldest sibling, Barbara Stahly (born in 1836), and the youngest, Daniel, born in 1856. The Elkhart Prairie was well-populated with Stahly descendants.

There were tragedies, of course. Between 1870 and 1880, nine cousins had been orphaned by the premature deaths of their parents: the six children of Barbara Stahly and John Ringenberg, and three children of Magdalena Stahly and Andrew Bleile.

Polly Stahly and her husband, Tobias Yoder, took in six of these orphans—an amazing and wonderful undertaking that deserves recognition.[4]

Spur Chart 8 (page 123) shows the siblings, their marriage partners, and their children.

Barbara Stahly married John Ringenberg in 1853, as has already been discussed. After her untimely death in 1869 and that of her husband in 1871, their six children were fostered in various homes of her relatives. Two of the six children married into the Smucker family, as did Barbara's brother, Daniel.

Pauline "Polly" Stahly married Tobias Yoder. They had no children; however Magdalena, Henry and Mary Anne Ringenberg, orphaned children of Polly's sister, Barbara, were fostered by Polly and Tobias. They also fostered Ezra, Ella, and Della Bleile, orphaned children of Magdalena Stahly and Andrew Bleile. After Tobias Yoder died in 1892, Polly married Christian Lantz. This couple lived in Howard County, Indiana, until Polly was widowed a second time, in 1919.

---

4   Family researchers are focused on descendants, sometimes to the neglect of those people who left no offspring, but whose contributions to the well-being of the family were immense, or whose stories are interesting in their own right.

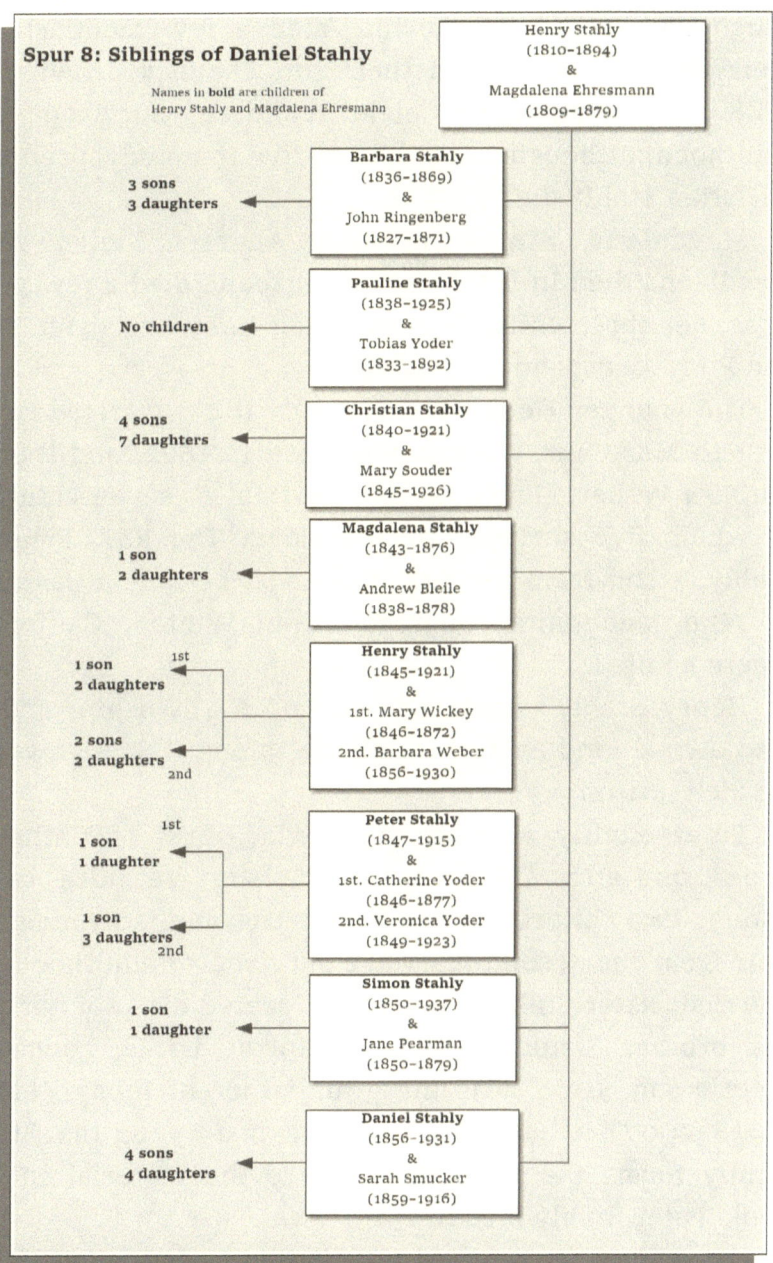

Spur 8: Siblings of Daniel Stahly

Names in bold are children of
Henry Stahly and Magdalena Ehresmann

Henry Stahly
(1810-1894)
&
Magdalena Ehresmann
(1809-1879)

3 sons
3 daughters ←

Barbara Stahly
(1836-1869)
&
John Ringenberg
(1827-1871)

No children ←

Pauline Stahly
(1838-1925)
&
Tobias Yoder
(1833-1892)

4 sons
7 daughters ←

Christian Stahly
(1840-1921)
&
Mary Souder
(1845-1926)

1 son
2 daughters ←

Magdalena Stahly
(1843-1876)
&
Andrew Bleile
(1838-1878)

1 son
2 daughters ← 1st

2 sons
2 daughters ← 2nd

Henry Stahly
(1845-1921)
&
1st. Mary Wickey
(1846-1872)
2nd. Barbara Weber
(1856-1930)

1 son
1 daughter ← 1st

1 son
3 daughters ← 2nd

Peter Stahly
(1847-1915)
&
1st. Catherine Yoder
(1846-1877)
2nd. Veronica Yoder
(1849-1923)

1 son
1 daughter ←

Simon Stahly
(1850-1937)
&
Jane Pearman
(1850-1879)

4 sons
4 daughters ←

Daniel Stahly
(1856-1931)
&
Sarah Smucker
(1859-1916)

Christian Stahly (born 1840) and his wife Mary Souder were the parents of eleven children. Their twin daughters, Elsina and Lovina, died a few months after their birth in 1880, and their son Chauncy drowned in 1888. The remaining eight children survived into adulthood, although some did not live to an advanced age. Christian Stahly died in 1921, age 81.

Magdalena Stahly married Andrew Bleile. After Magdalena died in 1876 and her husband died a few years later, her three children were taken in by her sister Polly and Polly's husband, Tobias Yoder.

The younger **Henry Stahly** (born 1845) married twice, first to Mary Ann Wickey, who died in 1872, and then to Barbara Weber. Henry fathered a total of seven children, of whom five survived to adulthood. The Rev. Emanuel Stahly, a son from the first marriage, became a pastor in the Old Mennonite congregation in Winton, California, where he died.

Henry Stahly's farm was in Locke Township, and he also owned land east of Nappanee, along U.S. Highway 6. He died in 1921.

Peter Stahly also married twice, first to Catherine Yoder, and after she died, to her sister, Veronica, called Fanny. Two children of the first marriage died young; the four from the second marriage survived to adulthood and married. Peter Stahly's farm was located directly north of his brother Daniel's, along SR19 in Locke Township. Peter's son, Irvin, was the grandfather of John I. Stahly (1938-2007), whose work on the history of the Stahly family forms the basis of much of the material in this book. Peter Stahly died in 1915.

Simon Stahly married Jean Pearman, who died at the birth of Sarah Alice Stahly in 1879. In 1902, Sarah married Simon Albrecht, whose brother, William Albrecht, married Alma Stahly, niece of Simon Stahly, in 1909. (Alma and Sarah were first cousins.)

Simon Stahly's eldest child was Daniel Stahly (1875–1960), who was named for his uncle.

Simon farmed acreage a few miles north of Nappanee. After he died in 1937, his obituary described him as having been the last surviving member of an old pioneer family in Elkhart County.

Daniel Stahly (born 1856) died of peritonitis in 1931. One sibling, Simon, survived him. The funeral was held in the First Mennonite Church, in Nappanee. This was the church (with a new name) in which his father and mother had become founding members in 1875. By the time of his death, all of his surviving children had married and he had numerous grandchildren.

Apparently, Daniel Stahly died without a will. The Locke Township farm passed to his second wife, Jeanette Brown, and, eventually, out of the family.

Family of Daniel Stahly and Sarah Smucker, circa 1910. Back row, from left: Harvey, Alma, Roy, Bertha, Ida. Front: Russell, Daniel, Sarah (née Smucker), Dorothy. Photo courtesy of William Kurtz.

Roy Stahly

Roy Stahly, born in 1893, was the fifth child of Daniel Stahly and Sarah Smucker. He grew up on the family farm in Locke Township, and joined the Mennonite Church on West Market Street. Where he met Ethel Frederick (born 1892) is not known, but most likely it was at school. Ethel's family was not Mennonite: it was associated with the Church of the Brethren. The "brick church"—the Union Center Church of the Brethren—across the road from the cemetery where so many Stahly family members had been buried, was the Fredericks' home church. The family farm was not far away.

Roy Stahly and Ethel Frederick were married in the Union Center Church of the Brethren on August 30, 1916, a few months before the death of Roy's mother, Sarah.

Before Roy could become Ethel's husband, her family required that he be baptized in the Church of the Brethren. In later life, Roy would joke that apparently the Brethren thought that the Mennonite baptism wasn't good enough.

Although the Mennonites and the Church of the Brethren are very similar in their beliefs and practices, they have different histories. Alexander Mack, the founder of the Church of the Brethren, had been influenced by the Lutheran Pietism movement and by Anabaptists. He was a religious exile from his native town of Schriesheim, near Heidelberg, leading a small group of believers first to Schwarzenau (Germany), then to the Netherlands, and, eventually, to Germantown, Pennsylvania.

One of the common names for the Church of the Brethren is the "Dunkard" church, which was derived from the denomination's insistence on a full-immersion baptism, accomplished by three forward-facing submersions of the individual's head. Mennonites used various forms of baptism, including water poured from a pitcher, immersion in a flowing stream, or a dunking one time backward. The form of baptism in the Mennonite church had been the cause of more than one schism over the years.

It is likely that the reason that Roy Stahly needed to be re-baptized in the Church of the Brethren, before his marriage, is that the Dunkards, or perhaps the Frederick family (who were staunch Dunkards), felt that the form used in Roy's original baptism, as an adult in the Mennonite church, was not correct.

Roy's marriage "outside the clan" of the Mennonite community did not seem to have caused any consternation among his family. It was not a big jump to go from the Mennonites to the Church of the Brethren. Relations between the two denominations were apparently friendly, at least in the Nappanee area. Occasionally, Mennonite funerals would be held at the Union Center church when Market Street was too muddy. The fact that the cemetery was across the road made it very convenient.

After they were married, the Stahly-Frederick family lived in Kosciusko County, south of Nappanee. The 1920 census indicates that the family was living on a farm in Scott Township. Frederick, their first child, was born in 1917; Donabelle was born in 1918. John Burton Stahly, the third child, was born in 1921.

Mainline Chart 8 (page 129) shows the Stahly-Frederick family.

In 1922, the Roy Stahly family acquired a farmstead in Sparta Township, Noble County, one county east of Elkhart County.

The farm was south of Ligonier, down a country road leading off U.S. Highway 33, near Eagle Lake. U.S. 33, also known as the Lincoln Highway, was an old route that originally ran northwest from Richmond, Virginia, to Niles, Michigan. The Elkhart River was nearby—the family remained on the Elkhart Prairie.

The Stahlys farmed on this property for almost 30 years. The Wawaka Church of the Brethren, about eight miles away, became the family's home church.

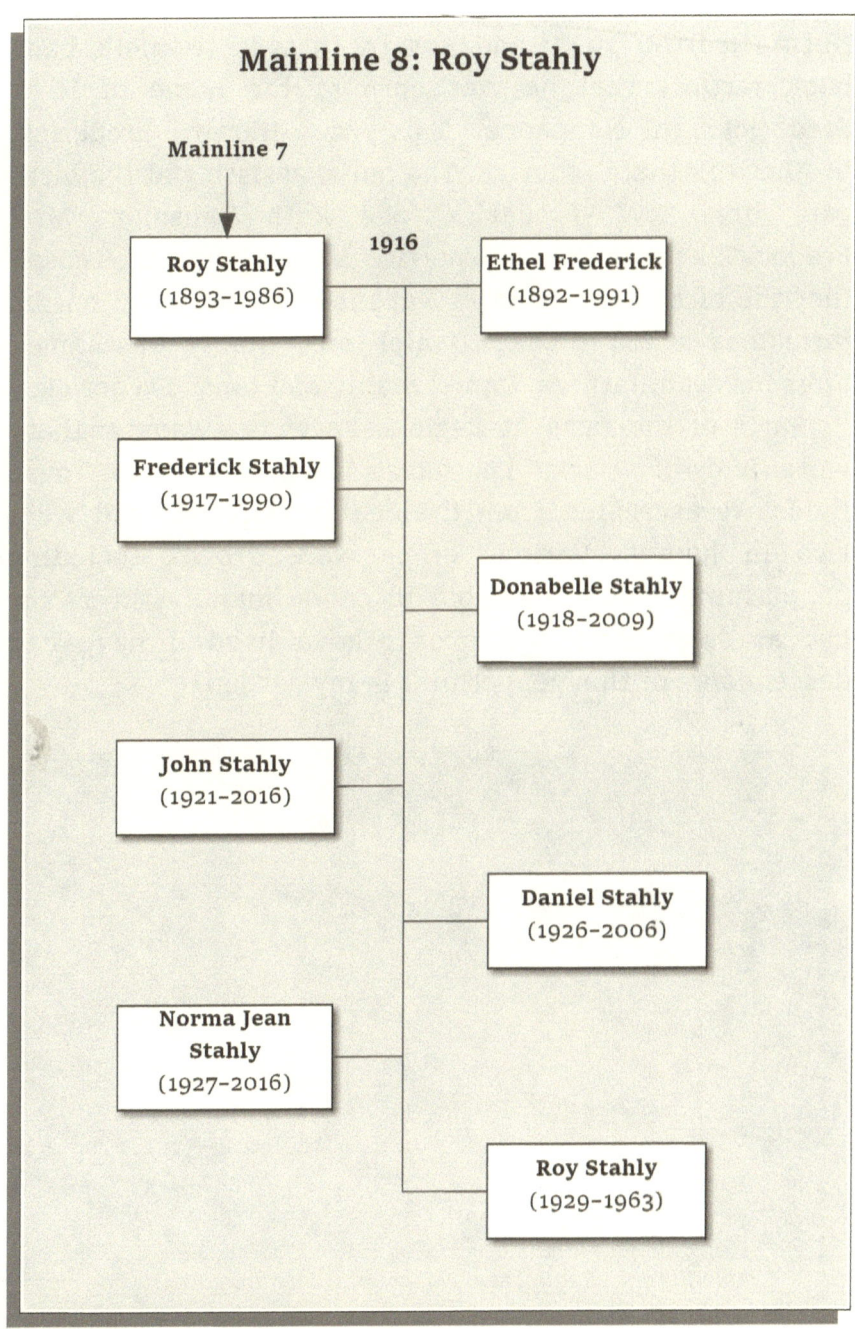

Mainline 8: Roy Stahly

Mainline 7

Roy Stahly
(1893–1986)

1916

Ethel Frederick
(1892–1991)

Frederick Stahly
(1917–1990)

Donabelle Stahly
(1918–2009)

John Stahly
(1921–2016)

Daniel Stahly
(1926–2006)

Norma Jean
Stahly
(1927–2016)

Roy Stahly
(1929–1963)

Three more children were born: Daniel Jonas in 1926; Norma Jean in 1927; and Roy Jr, in 1929. Daniel's baby book records that he was born at the home of H.W. Frederick, in Nappanee. This was Harvey Frederick, brother of Ethel Frederick. The nurse assisting at the birth was Mrs. H.W. Frederick, née Ruth Dausman. Mrs. Frederick's professional expertise was no doubt the reason that the birth took place in Nappanee, rather than on the farmstead at Eagle Lake. Daniel Jonas Stahly was named after his grandfathers, Daniel Stahly and Jonas Frederick.

Parts of the farm at Eagle Lake were swampy: there were fields of "muck," i.e., moist, black, fertile soil. These fields were created from drained swampland, and were rich in humus. Various crops were grown, including peppermint, which was sold to candy manufacturers for use as sweetener. Wherever I have lived, I have had descendants of this peppermint in my garden.

Stahly Farm at Eagle Lake, Noble Co., (date unknown)

Potatoes were also grown. In 1947, Roy Stahly was named "Potato King" for Indiana, having achieved a record harvest of 712 bushels of No.1 potatoes per acre from a 12 acre field of muck. At the 1947 northern Indiana muck-growers exhibition, Roy won blue ribbons for that year's potatoes.

The children went to elementary school in nearby Kimmell, a three mile walk each way. The high school was at Cromwell.

During WW2, German POWs were brought in by train from a camp in Fort Wayne to work on the farm.[5] The younger children remembered that the POWs wore striped uniforms, and that the kids were required to stay in the yard while the prisoners were working.

In later life, Roy Stahly occasionally reminisced with his grandchildren that he could understand and speak with a few of the POWs. Roy had learned a little German from his father, Daniel, likely a dialect that was used in the Pfalz. When and how Henry Stahly, the emigrant, had learned English is not known, but a German dialect was certainly his first language. His obituary states that his funeral was preached in both English and German.

Amish-Mennonite services used German dialect in the early years. One contentious point between more conservative-minded congregations of the Amish-Mennonites and the more reform-minded ones was whether Sunday services could, with propriety, be conducted in English.

---

5   This was Fort Scott, where about 600 German prisoners were interned starting in late 1944. Most came from Rommel's *Afrika Korps*, and had been captured during the campaigns in north Africa in 1943.

The Amish and Mennonites from Pennsylvania spoke their own dialect, using it as one way to keep themselves isolated from the modern world. Today, the Old Order Amish still use the traditional language.

Frederick

Ethel Frederick's parents were Jonas Frederick and Lydia Anglemeyer. Spur Chart 9 (page 133) shows their ancestors. Because of the complicated interconnections of the Frederick family and the Anglemeyer family, names of spouses are not shown on this chart, except when necessary to show the actual line of descent.

Jonas's parents, Sarah Anglemeyer and William Frederick, were living in Ohio, in Hardin County, according to the 1860 U.S. Federal Census. In an article in a biographical history of Elkhart County, Jonas is described as a former schoolteacher and a member of the German Baptist Church, i.e., the Church of the Brethren. Jonas moved to Elkhart County in 1872. In 1873, he married Lydia Anglemeyer, who was his first cousin, once removed.

Jonas' father, William Frederick, died in 1880 in Hardin County in the explosion of a threshing machine. Jonas' mother remained in Hardin County, where William Frederick had come to work in the coal mines. William had been born in about 1832 in Columbiana County, Ohio, on the eastern edge of the state.

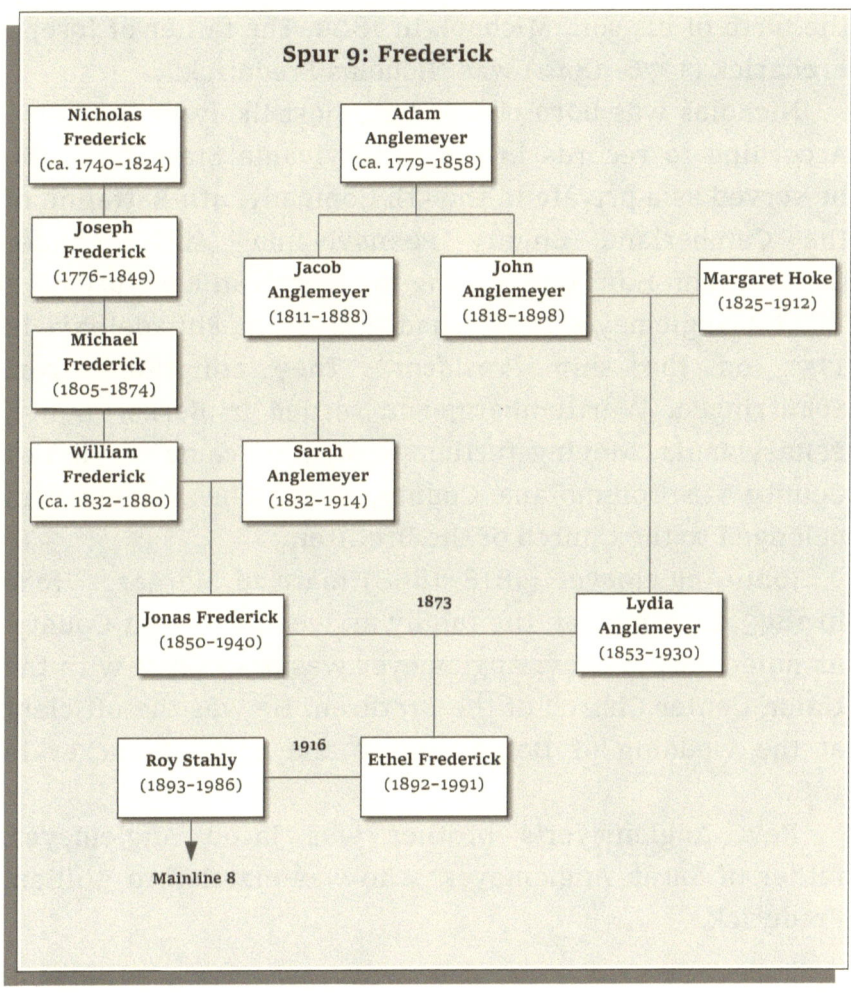

Spur 9: Frederick

Nicholas Frederick (ca. 1740–1824)

Adam Anglemeyer (ca. 1779–1858)

Joseph Frederick (1776–1849)

Jacob Anglemeyer (1811–1888)

John Anglemeyer (1818–1898)

Margaret Hoke (1825–1912)

Michael Frederick (1805–1874)

William Frederick (ca. 1832–1880)

Sarah Anglemeyer (1832–1914)

Jonas Frederick (1850–1940)

1873

Lydia Anglemeyer (1853–1930)

Roy Stahly (1893–1986)

1916

Ethel Frederick (1892–1991)

Mainline 8

William's father, Michael Frederick (1805-1874), had lived in Columbiana County his entire life. Michael, who was married to Elizabeth Fox, was the son of Joseph Frederick and Mary Crubaugh. Joseph was born in Westmoreland County, Pennsylvania, in 1776. Apparently he came to Ohio, along with his father, sometime before the birth of his son, Michael, in 1805. The father of Joseph Frederick (1776-1849) was Nicholas Frederick.

Nicholas was born circa 1740, most likely in Germany. According to records in the Pennsylvania State Archives, he served as a private in the 5th Company, 4th Battalion of the Cumberland County Pennsylvania Militia, under Captain John Hamilton, during the American Revolution.

The Anglemeyer family had arrived in Philadelphia in 1752 on the ship *President*.[6] They emigrated from Schützingen, Württemberg, and settled in Berks County, Pennsylvania. Moving further west, they came to Elkhart County via Columbiana County, Ohio. The Anglemeyers belonged to the Church of the Brethren.

John Anglemeyer (1818-1898) married Margaret Hoke in 1843, and in 1854, the family arrived in Elkhart County. As noted earlier, Rev. Anglemeyer was associated with the Union Center Church of the Brethren. He was the officiant at the wedding of Daniel Stahly and Sarah Smucker in 1880.

Rev. Anglemeyer's brother was Jacob Anglemeyer, father of Sarah Anglemeyer, who was married to William Frederick.

---

6   This surname is sometimes spelled "Anglemyer." I use "Anglemeyer," which is what I found on the tombstone of the Rev. John Anglemeyer at Union Center Cemetery.

Lydia Anglemeyer was born in 1853 in Columbiana County, Ohio. The Fredericks and the Anglemeyers both had farmsteads in Union Township, not far from the Church of the Brethren at Union Center. Lydia and Jonas Frederick would have known each other from church, but there were already close family connections when the couple married in 1873. A total of nine children were born between 1875 and 1892.

Ethel Frederick graduated from Nappanee High School in 1912, and enrolled in a teacher certification program. She taught young children (kindergarten or first grade) until her marriage in 1916. Female teachers at that time were not allowed to be married.

Lydia Frederick, née Anglemeyer, died in 1930; Jonas lived another ten years. One of his grandchildren, Jean Stahly, remembered being sent after her grandfather, who sometimes wandered away from the farm at Eagle Lake. In his old age, Jonas had a long, white beard, which the younger children found scary.

There are many descendants of Jonas Frederick and Lydia Anglemeyer. Except for those of Ethel Frederick, their stories are not included in this book.

Jonas Frederick Family, circa 1898. Back row, from left: Frances, Jesse, Anna, John, Edith, Franklin. Front: Jonas, Ethel, Jude, Harvey, Lydia (née Anglemeyer).

Roy Stahly's Siblings

When Roy Stahly moved to Noble County in 1922, his siblings, with one exception, remained in Elkhart County, or nearby.

Spur Chart 10 (page 137) shows Roy's siblings, their marriage partners, and the number and gender of their offspring.

Harvey Stahly married Nellie McGowen in 1904, and they had four sons. Nellie was the daughter of James McGowen, long-time pastor at the Market Street church.

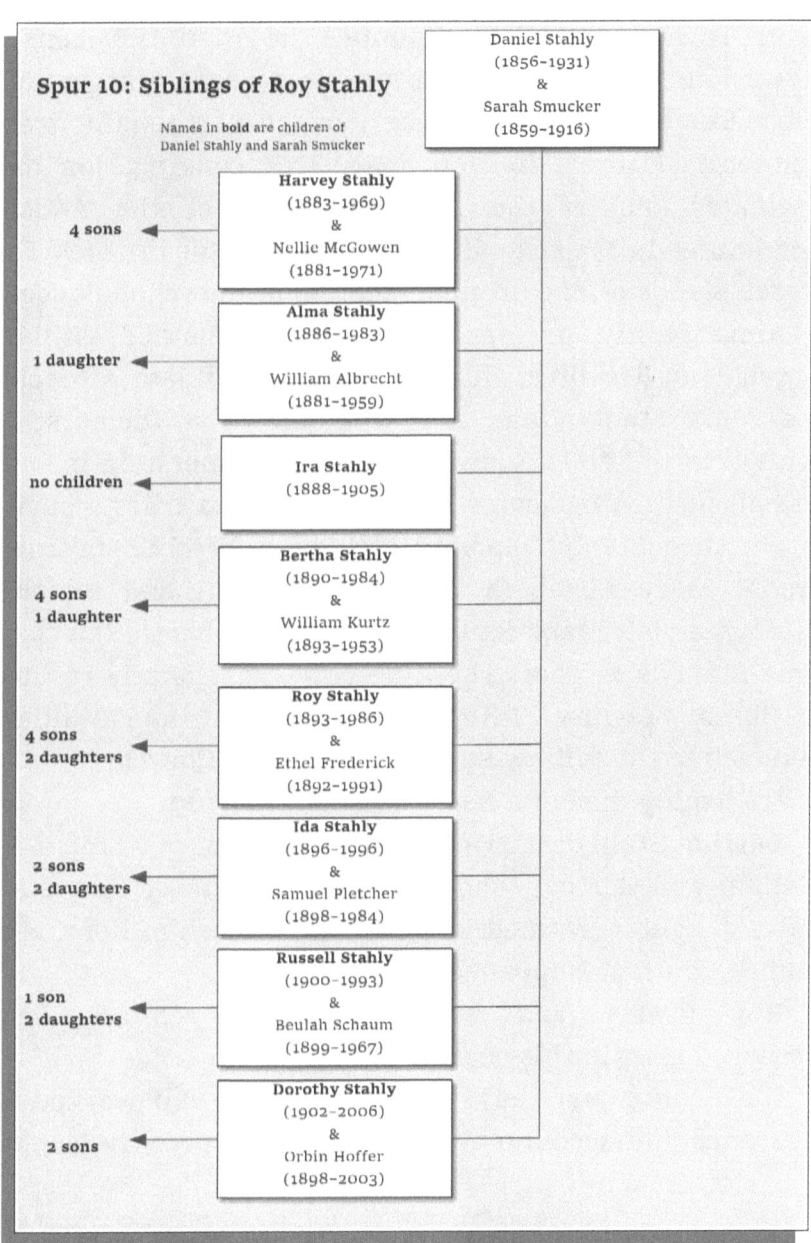

Spur 10: Siblings of Roy Stahly

Names in **bold** are children of
Daniel Stahly and Sarah Smucker

Daniel Stahly
(1856–1931)
&
Sarah Smucker
(1859–1916)

Harvey Stahly
(1883–1969)
&
Nellie McGowen
(1881–1971)

4 sons

Alma Stahly
(1886–1983)
&
William Albrecht
(1881–1959)

1 daughter

Ira Stahly
(1888–1905)

no children

Bertha Stahly
(1890–1984)
&
William Kurtz
(1893–1953)

4 sons
1 daughter

Roy Stahly
(1893–1986)
&
Ethel Frederick
(1892–1991)

4 sons
2 daughters

Ida Stahly
(1896–1996)
&
Samuel Pletcher
(1898–1984)

2 sons
2 daughters

Russell Stahly
(1900–1993)
&
Beulah Schaum
(1899–1967)

1 son
2 daughters

Dorothy Stahly
(1902–2006)
&
Orbin Hoffer
(1898–2003)

2 sons

McGowen had preached the English part of Henry Stahly's funeral in 1894. The Harvey Stahly farm was in Locke Township, Elkhart County. The 1930 U.S. census shows four sons at home with their parents. Harvey and Nettie Stahly were both members of the North Main Street Mennonite Church, in Nappanee. This congregation had originated out of the early meetings of the Amish-Mennonites in the schoolhouse that was built in 1867. The church stands on the original location of the schoolhouse.

Alma Stahly, as mentioned earlier, married William Albrecht, of Tiskilwa, Illinois, in 1909. William Albrecht, like Alma Stahly, was a descendant of a Diemerstein family,[7] in the Pfalz. Considering that Diemerstein is such a small place, this seems noteworthy. Alma's first cousin, Sarah Alice Stahly, married William Albrecht's brother, Simon. Mary Elizabeth Albrecht, William and Simon's sister, married Frank Smucker, brother of Sarah Smucker, Alma Stahly's mother. The Albrecht/Stahly family resided in Bureau County, Illinois, where Alma and William belonged to the Willow Springs Mennonite Church.

Ira Stahly died of a heart ailment at age 17.

Bertha Stahly married William Kurtz, of Nappanee. William and Bertha, who were the parents of four sons and a daughter, farmed in Jefferson Township, Kosciusko County, south of Nappanee.

Roy Stahly and Ethel Frederick's children are discussed later in this chapter.

Ida Stahly married Samuel Pletcher, who worked in insurance and accountancy in Elkhart County. The couple

---

7   William Albrecht's ancestor, Christian Albrecht, son of Johannes Albrecht and Magdalena Güngerich, married Elisabeth Engel, who was born in about 1781. The Engel family was from Diemerstein.

remained members of the Mennonite church. Both Ida and Samuel are buried in the cemetery at Yellow Creek Mennonite Church, west of Goshen. They were the parents of two sons and two daughters, all of whom survived to adulthood.

Russell Stahly's first wife was Beulah Schaum, whom he married in 1920. Of their three children. their son died as a baby in an accident caused by a runaway horse. Russell and Beulah farmed in Union Township. After Beulah died in 1967, Russell married a second time. In 1977, he was again widowed, and he took a third wife in 1980. This wife also died, making Russell a widower for the third time. Russell Stahly died in 1993, and was survived by his fourth wife.

Dorothy Stahly married Orbin "Jack" Hoffer in 1921. In 2001, they celebrated their 80th wedding anniversary, and were recognized as being the couple in Indiana that had been married the longest, at that time. Dorothy and Jack were the parents of two sons, and resided south of Nappanee, in Scott Township, Kosciusko County. Their house was not far from Dorothy's sister, Bertha. Jack and Dorothy belonged to the family church, the First Mennonite Church, of Nappanee. Jack Hoffer died in 2002 at 104 years old; Dorothy died, also 104 years old, in 2006.

After Eagle Lake

Roy and Ethel's children, born between 1917 and 1929, produced 24 grandchildren. After leaving the Eagle Lake farm, Roy and Ethel Stahly moved to a bungalow on East 6th Street in Ligonier, still remaining on the Elkhart Prairie. Roy worked part-time at a hardware store, at the library, and he helped out on the farms where four of his six children lived. Ethel's specialty, butterscotch pie, was generously distributed to her children and grandchildren.

Roy Stahly died in 1986, 301 years after the 1685 birth of his great-great-great-grandfather in Sigriswil, Switzerland. Ethel died in 1991. Both are buried in Oak Park Cemetery in Ligonier.

Roy Stahly Family, circa 1933. Back, from left, Fred, Daniel, Jean, Donabelle. Front, John, Roy, Roy Jr., Ethel (née Frederick).

*

For the purposes of this history, this is the end of the line. Of course, as there are many people who descend from Roy Stahly and Ethel Frederick, this ending is entirely arbitrary. In fact, the lines go on—quite robustly. Brief sketches of the children of Roy and Ethel Stahly follow.

Fred Stahly (1917-1990) married Doris Knepper (1919-2005) in 1940. Doris was the daughter of Walter and Alice Knepper, who lived in the southern part of Noble County. Fred was a WW2 veteran and became the Standard Oil distributor for the Ligonier area, where they raised three sons.

Donabelle Stahly (1918-2009) married Earnest Shell (1918-2010) in 1941 in the Wawaka Church of the Brethren. Earnest was the son of John and Etta Shell. Donabelle and Ernie Shell, along with their daughter and two sons, lived on a farm south of Ligonier, not far from where Donabelle had grown up on the Eagle Lake farm.

John Stahly (1921-2016) and Edith Ott (1922-1979) were married in 1940. Edith was the daughter of Clint and Edna Ott. After John served in WW2, the couple settled in South Bend, where John worked in the engineering department at the Bendix Corporation. Five children were born, four sons and a daughter. After Edith died in 1979, John married Rose Stahly, née Dull, widow of John's youngest brother, Roy Jr.

Daniel Stahly (1926–2006) married Mabel Wright (1926–2016) in Cromwell in 1946. She was the daughter of Clarence and Anna Wright, who lived on a farm west of Cromwell. After farming for about 12 years on a farm north of Albion, Indiana, Dan became the Standard Oil (Amoco) distributor for Tipton County, Indiana, where the family (two daughters, two sons) relocated in 1965.

Jean Stahly (1927–2016) and John Loveless (1925–2002) lived on a dairy farm north of Cromwell, Sparta Township, Noble County, where they raised prize Guernseys. Jean and John (the son of Arthur and Marie Loveless) were married in 1948. For many years, Jean was the nurse for the West Noble school system. Jean and John were the parents of three sons and three daughters.

Roy Stahly Jr (1929–1963) married Rosalind Dull (1929–2012) in 1949. Her parents were Arnold and Nolene Dull. Together with their children—two sons and a daughter—they lived on a farm near Middlebury, Indiana, until Roy Jr. died in a farm accident in 1963. Rose married her late husband's elder brother, John, in 1980.

The following article appeared in the *Nappanee Advance-News* on July 3, 1907.

STAHLY FAMILY REUNION
Held at The Home of Peter H. Stahly
Last Saturday—Large Attendance

The second annual reunion of the Stahly family was held at the home of Peter H. Stahly just north of Nappanee last Saturday, June 29th.

The attendance was good, there being 254 persons present, who participated in or enjoyed a splendid program arranged by the program committee, as follows:

Song--"All Hail the Power of Jesus' Name"...Audience

Invocation....................................Rev. David Metzler

Song--"What a Friend we Have in Jesus"......Audience

Address of Welcome........................Mrs. Edw. Lape

Song...Children

Recitation--"Be Careful What You Say"......Roy Stahly

Recitation--"Book of Memory".............Mary Emmert

Recitation—"Country Life"......................Elva Shrock

Talk--"Our Motive in Family Reunions".....D. J. Stahly

Octet—Carrie Ringenberg, Nellie Stahly, Celesta Garber, Cora Weldy, Geo. Peters, Harvey Stahly, Ed Lape, and Jess Stahly

Recitation--"The Skeptic's Daughter"....Inez Smucker

Recitation--"My Welcome Beyond"........Lona Strauss

Song...Audience

Recitation--"Strength for To-day".......Blanche Geyer
Recitation--"Country Cousins"........Hazel Ringenberg
Recitation--"Little Things".......................Vera Stahly
Quartet--....Cora Miller Stahly, Iva Stahly, Clayton
   Stahly and John Weldy
History of the Stahly Family
Miscellaneous Business
Song--"God be With You Till We Meet Again"...........
....Audience

There are over 600 descendants of the Stahly family
engaged in the various pursuits in life, and scattered
from Massachusetts to California; and from North
Dakota to Arkansas and Oklahoma.

The following officers were elected for the ensuing
year: Henry Ringenberg, president; Peter H. Stahly,
vice-president; C. J. Stahly, secretary and treasurer.
The time and place for holding the next reunion is to
be determined by a committee appointed for that
purpose.

5. The Menno Game

From their earliest times, the actual number of Amish-Mennonites of Swiss extraction has been very small, relative to the larger population around them. This was true in Switzerland, and in their places of refuge—Alsace, the Pfalz, the Netherlands, and North America.

Other groups of Mennonites, in Galacia or Russia, for example, were also very small relative to the dominate culture in which they lived.

Non-conformist religious beliefs and a history of being persecuted contributed to the Amish-Mennonites' tendency to "stick together." These insular instincts meant that often the choice of a marriage partner came from a small pool of candidates: who was nearby of the appropriate age, who was available, and who held the "correct" religious beliefs.[1]

Among   Swiss   Amish-Mennonite   families,   this clannishness   created   a   complex   web   of   interconnected families. People of Amish-Mennonite heritage sometimes amuse   themselves   by   playing   the   Menno   Game,   an Anabaptist   interpretation   of   the   "six   degrees   of separation" idea.

To play the game, at least two players with surnames of Swiss Amish-Mennonite heritage work out how many generations it takes before they can uncover a common ancestor. Often, of course, they discover that they are related in one or more ways, either by blood or marriage.

To be successful in the Menno Game, it is usually only necessary to connect to one of the old Amish-Mennonite families in early Pennsylvania. These "gateway" families are similar to European royalty: a connection to one of them means there is likely a connection to many of them.

---

1   This sort of clannishness is not, of course, unusual. In the era before mass travel and communication, marriage partners among common folk were almost always selected from within a few miles of where a person lived. The aristocracy tended to select their marriage partners for dynastic, political, or economic reasons.

A partial list of these "gateway" surnames includes:

Beachy

Birkey

Det(t)weiler

Gingerich

Hostetler

Kauffman

Lehman

Mast

Miller

Mishler

Nafziger

Oesch (Eash)

Smucker

Stoltzfus

Stutzman

Troyer

Yoder

Zimmerman

Zook

One notable feature of this list is that every name (except Stoltzfus) is of Swiss origin. When a surname has been altered from its original form, the North American spelling is used here.

The Stahly family discussed in this book is connected to many of these families through Sarah Smucker (1859–1916). She is the gateway person through whom all of her descendants are related to a vast number of Amish-

Mennonite cousins. For Stahly participants in the Menno Game, she is the key person.

Spur Charts 11 (page 150) and 12 (page 154) show these connections. On Spur Chart 11, starting with Sarah Smucker at the bottom of the page and moving upward, different lines eventually lead to six different Amish-Mennonite patriarchs: Christian Schmucker, Nicholas Stolzfuss, Christian Müller, Christian Joder, Moritz Zug, and Michael Troyer. In addition to these six, two additional patriarchs are shown on Spur Chart 12: Christian Stutzmann and Jacob Hochstetler.

A very brief history of each of these families follows. (Christian Schmucker, Sarah's paternal ancestor, has already been discussed in Chapter 4.) Others have researched these families, for the most part. As usual, many of the surnames have changed from their original spellings.

Nicholas Stolzfuss (or Stoltzfus) is unusual for an Amish-Mennonite patriarch, in that his ancestors were not Swiss. He was born in Germany in 1718. His paternal ancestors had been Lutheran pastors in Thuringia, where the surname was sometimes written as "Steltzfuss." In 1717, his father, Christoph, became a citizen of Zweibrücken. After Christoph died, Nicholas was sent to work on a local farm, where his co-workers were Amish. He converted, married, and fathered two children, Barbara and Christian. In 1766, the family emigrated to Pennsylvania on the ship *Polly*.

Today, people with the surname "Stoltzfus" descend from this family. The Nicholas Stolzfuss family house is still standing in Wyomissing, Pennsylvania.

Barbara Stolzfuss, daughter of Nicholas, was born in Europe, and came to Pennsylvania along with her brother, Christian, and her father. Barbara married Johannes (John) Schmucker, the son of immigrant Christian Schmucker, who was living in Lancaster County. In 1787, Barbara Stolzfuss and her husband acquired 500 acres of land in Berks County from her brother.

Christian Müller, which became "Miller" in North America, was born in Switzerland, circa 1708. His son Hannes—John—was born about 1730 at La Sagneule, Neuchâtel. John Miller married Magdalena Lehman. The family was a neighbor to the Jacob Hochstetler family at the first Amish settlement in Pennsylvania, at Northkill. There are many Amish-Mennonite families in North America with the Miller surname—not all descend from this line.

The Joder (i.e., Yoder) family is from Steffisburg, Canton Bern. Steffisburg is a few kilometers from Sigriswil, north of Thun. The Joders were a very large clan, and had evolved into Reformed, Amish and Mennonite branches. **Christian Joder,** in the Amish branch, was born in Europe, and emigrated to Pennsylvania in 1742 on board the *Francis and Elizabeth*, along with other members of his family.

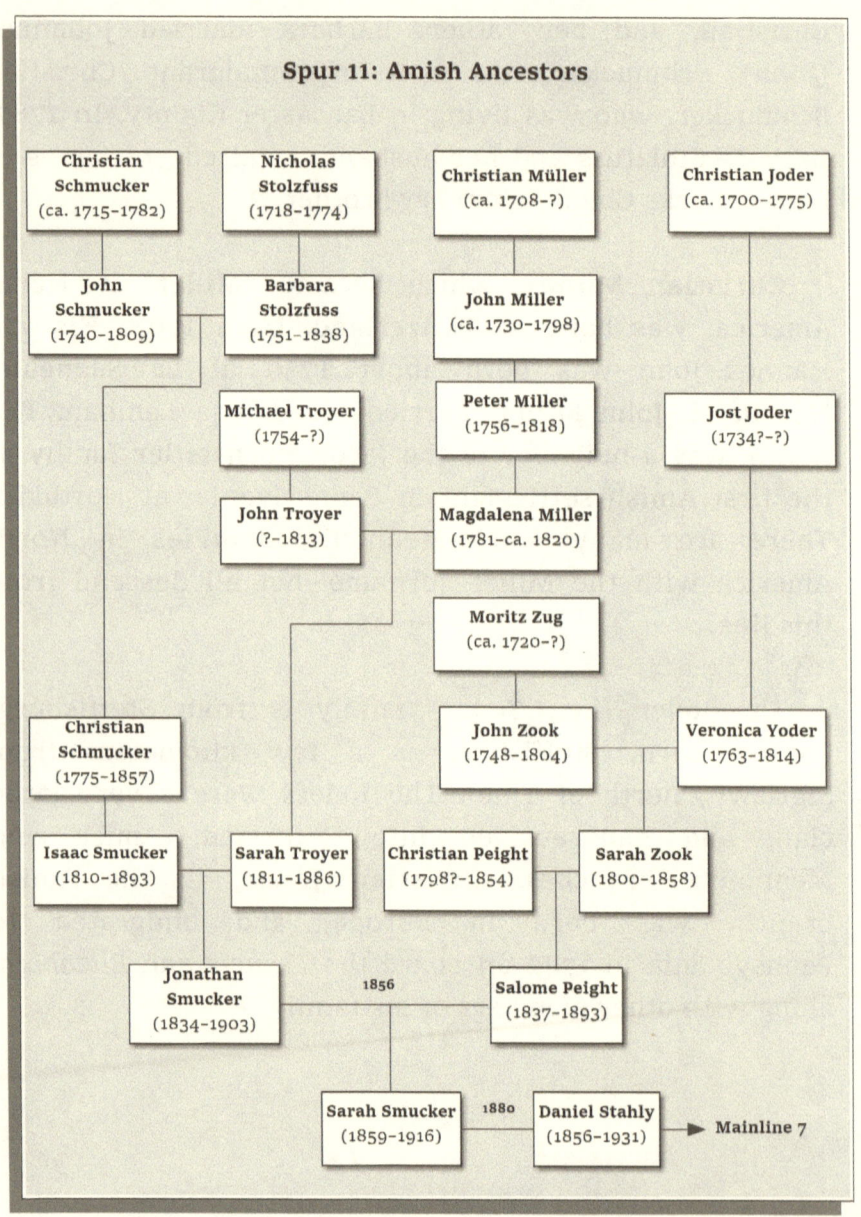

Spur 11: Amish Ancestors

Christian Schmucker (ca. 1715–1782)

Nicholas Stolzfuss (1718–1774)

Christian Müller (ca. 1708–?)

Christian Joder (ca. 1700–1775)

John Schmucker (1740–1809)

Barbara Stolzfuss (1751–1838)

John Miller (ca. 1730–1798)

Michael Troyer (1754–?)

Peter Miller (1756–1818)

Jost Joder (1734?–?)

John Troyer (?–1813)

Magdalena Miller (1781–ca. 1820)

Moritz Zug (ca. 1720–?)

Christian Schmucker (1775–1857)

John Zook (1748–1804)

Veronica Yoder (1763–1814)

Isaac Smucker (1810–1893)

Sarah Troyer (1811–1886)

Christian Peight (1798?–1854)

Sarah Zook (1800–1858)

Jonathan Smucker (1834–1903)

1856

Salome Peight (1837–1893)

Sarah Smucker (1859–1916)

1880

Daniel Stahly (1856–1931)

➤ Mainline 7

Although the Joder/Yoder genealogy has been extensively researched, there is a gap in what is known about the 1742 emigrants. They descended from one of the sons of Jost Joder (born ca. 1607) and Anna Trachsel, of Steffisburg—which precise son is uncertain. The Joder/Trachsel couple had 12 children, many of whom married and disappeared from Steffisburg in the 1690s. Some went to Alsace, some went to the Pfalz. One son, Caspar Joder, born 1664, went to the Langenberg estate, which was a neighbor to St. Germanshof, where the Stähli family lived 100 years later.

Steffisburg was a center of Anabaptist dissent. In addition to the Joder family, other well-known Amish-Mennonite families came from this village. Kauffmann, Zimmermann, Blanck, Rupp, and Reusser are Anabaptist surnames frequently found in the Steffisburg parish register. By 1700, almost all of the Anabaptist families had left Steffisburg.

In Elkhart County, members of the Stahly and Yoder families intermarried on several occasions.[2]

Two of Daniel Stahly's (1856–1931) siblings took Yoder spouses: Polly married Tobias Yoder in 1857, and Peter married, in succession, two Yoder sisters, Catherine and Veronica.

---

2 In 1684, in Steffisburg, Jacob Joder married Margareth Stähli. She was from the Stähli clan in Oberhofen, and thus not related to the family in Sigriswil. Today, some of the Joders who live in Steffisburg are descended from this couple, which was not Anabaptist.

The Troyer family originated in Trub, in the Emmental, Canton Bern, where the name was written as "Dreier" or "Treyer." Michael Troyer emigrated to Lancaster County, and married Magdalena Mast. They lived in Somerset County, Pennsylvania. Their son, the younger **Michael Troyer**, born in 1754, married Anna Rickenbach. The next generation was John Troyer, who married Magdalena Miller, of the Miller family, and who was also a descendant of the Stutzmann family.

Steffisburg. ☻ *Jakob Samuel Weibel (1771–1846).*
(Swiss National Library)

Moritz Zug ("Zaugg" or "Zook") was likely born on the Wilensteinerhof in about 1720. This farming estate is near Trippstadt and the Aschbacherhof, where the Stähli family had lived for a time. There were several Zaugg families in Canton Bern. This branch resided in the Emmental, where Moritz Zug's ancestors were baptized in Trub and Rüderswil before the family relocated to the Pfalz. Moritz Zug came to Philadelphia on board the ship *Francis and Elizabeth* in 1742, along with his brothers.

Moritz Zug's son, John Zook (1748–1804), married Veronica Yoder, daughter of Jost Joder (born ca. 1734), of the Christian Joder family.

The next two families, the Stutzmanns and the Hochstetlers are on Spur Chart 12 (page 154).

These two families were neighbors in the Northkill Amish settlement, and were linked by marriage: **Christian Stutzmann** had married Barbara Hochstetler. Their son, the younger Christian Stutzman (1758–1825), married Elizabeth Steiner. Elizabeth Stutzman, daughter of the younger Christian Stutzman and Elizabeth Steiner, was the first wife of Christian Schmucker, grandson of the emigrant Christian Schmucker.

Meanwhile, Mary Stutzman (the double 'n' had become a single 'n'), sister of the younger Christian Stutzman, married Peter Miller, of the Miller family. By these means were Isaac Smucker and Sarah Troyer second cousins when they became husband and wife.

Spur 12: Amish Ancestors, continued

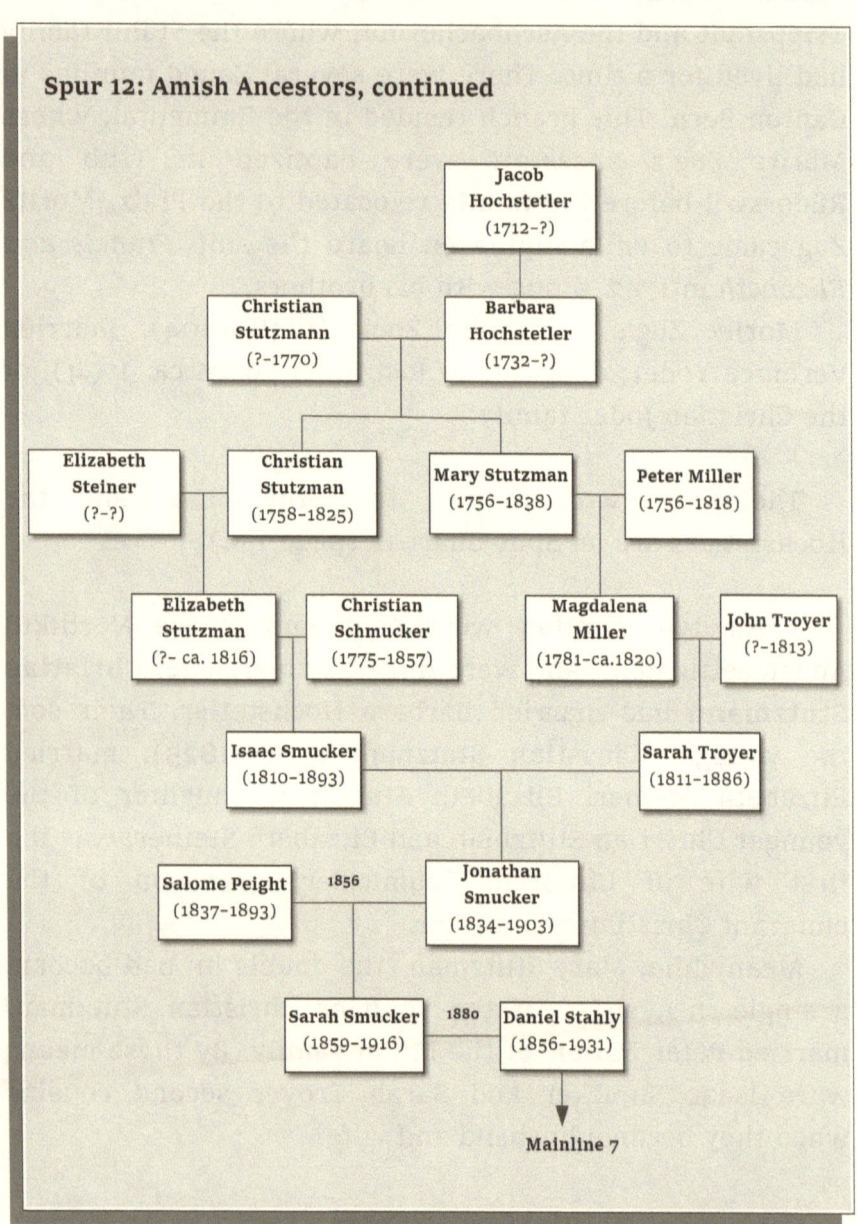

Jacob Hochstetler (1712–?)

Christian Stutzmann (?–1770) — Barbara Hochstetler (1732–?)

Elizabeth Steiner (?–?)

Christian Stutzman (1758–1825) — Mary Stutzman (1756–1838) — Peter Miller (1756–1818)

Elizabeth Stutzman (?– ca. 1816) — Christian Schmucker (1775–1857)

Magdalena Miller (1781–ca.1820) — John Troyer (?–1813)

Isaac Smucker (1810–1893) — Sarah Troyer (1811–1886)

Salome Peight (1837–1893) — 1856 — Jonathan Smucker (1834–1903)

Sarah Smucker (1859–1916) — 1880 — Daniel Stahly (1856–1931)

Mainline 7

Jacob Hochstetler (in North America, often written as "Hostetler") was born in Ste. Marie-aux-Mines, Alsace, in 1712. He emigrated on board the ship *Charming Nancy* in 1738, and helped to establish the Amish settlement at Northkill, which was the first of its kind in Pennsylvania.

During the French and Indian War (1754–1763), the family was attacked by the local indigenous inhabitants. The reason for the attack is not certain. It could have been related to the war between the French and the English, or it may have been more personal.

Several members of the Hochstetler family—Jacob's wife and two young children—were killed in the attack, and Jacob and two of his sons were taken captive. A widely circulated story said that Jacob Hochstetler would not let his sons defend the family with firearms, due to his belief in the Amish-Mennonite tenet of non-violence. This story became a standard feature of Amish-Mennonite Sunday schools.

Jacob Hochstetler escaped from his captors, and his sons were eventually released. His daughter, Barbara, had married Christian Stutzmann by the time of the attack, and the couple was living on a neighboring farm.

With the large number of children typical of Amish-Mennonite families, these eight patriarchs are the ancestors of many people. Descendants of Sarah Smucker and Daniel Stahly are related to all of them, and to many others who remain undiscovered.

*

The kerfuffle (if that is what it was) caused by the baptism/re-baptism issue when Roy Stahly and Ethel Frederick were married in 1916 becomes more understandable when the heritage of the Frederick and Anglemeyer families is examined. These branches of two old Pennsylvania families, both of German extraction, were associated with the Church of the Brethren. And it turns out that Ethel Frederick was a descendant of the church's founder, **Alexander Mack**.

The Church of the Brethren grew out of a movement initiated in Germany by Alexander Mack (1679–1735) in the early part of the 18th century. He had been born into a prosperous family of millers in the German town of Schriesheim. This village is situated between the Rhine in the west, and the Odenwald, a wooded upland district, in the east.

Today, the west-facing slopes of the Odenwald are planted as vineyards. The Rhine plain is primarily agricultural. The Schriesheim *Altstadt* (old quarter) retains some fine half-timbered buildings, including the old *Rathaus,* on the town square, where the Mack family house also once stood. A small stream running down from the Odenwald hills powered the numerous mills that had provided an economic basis for the town. The ruin of the Strahlenburg above the village creates a romantic atmosphere.

After Schriesheim was depopulated by the Thirty Years' War, Swiss immigrants had helped to re-settle the town. It was beginning to recover when death and destruction again devastated the village.

The Nine Years' War (1688-1697) brought successive waves of invading French troops to the region. Schriesheim, like nearby Heidelberg, was plundered and burned.

Mack was born in the middle of this turmoil. His ancestors had been mayors of Schriesheim, and Mack, as a younger son, had expected to attend the university in Heidelberg. After one of his elder brothers died, however, Mack took over the operation of the family's mill.

Influenced by Pietists and Anabaptists, Mack began to hold illegal religious meetings. After a brush with the local authorities, he went into exile in Schwarzenau, near the present-day town of Bad Berleburg, in the modern German state of North Rhine-Westphalia. His wife, children, and a small group of followers went with him.

Schriesheim, circa 1845

When conditions there made further emigration necessary, Mack and his flock went to East Friesland, in the Netherlands, in 1720. Economic pressure resulted in a further emigration to Germantown, Pennsylvania, in 1729, where an earlier group of Brethren had already settled.

Like the Anabaptists, the Brethren (Dunkards, as they were sometimes called) eschewed infant baptism, asserted the primacy of the New Testament, believed in a creed of non-violence, and held that adult individuals alone are enabled to make decisions about their religious lives, unhindered by social, political or ecclesiastical institutions.

Although it had not been Alexander Mack's intention to start a new denomination, the Church of the Brethren took hold in North America, especially in the eastern part of Pennsylvania. As settlers spread westward to Ohio and Indiana, they took their church with them.

Alexander Mack married Anna Margaretha Kling in Schriesheim in 1701. Johannes, their second son, was born in 1703 and was baptized in the Reformed church there.

Johannes Mack married Anna Schneider in the Netherlands in 1725, and the couple went to Germantown with the other emigrants in 1729. Their son, Alexander Mack III, was born in Germantown. He was the father of Sarah Mack (born 1775), who married Daniel Longenecker in 1799, as shown on Spur Chart 13, page 159.

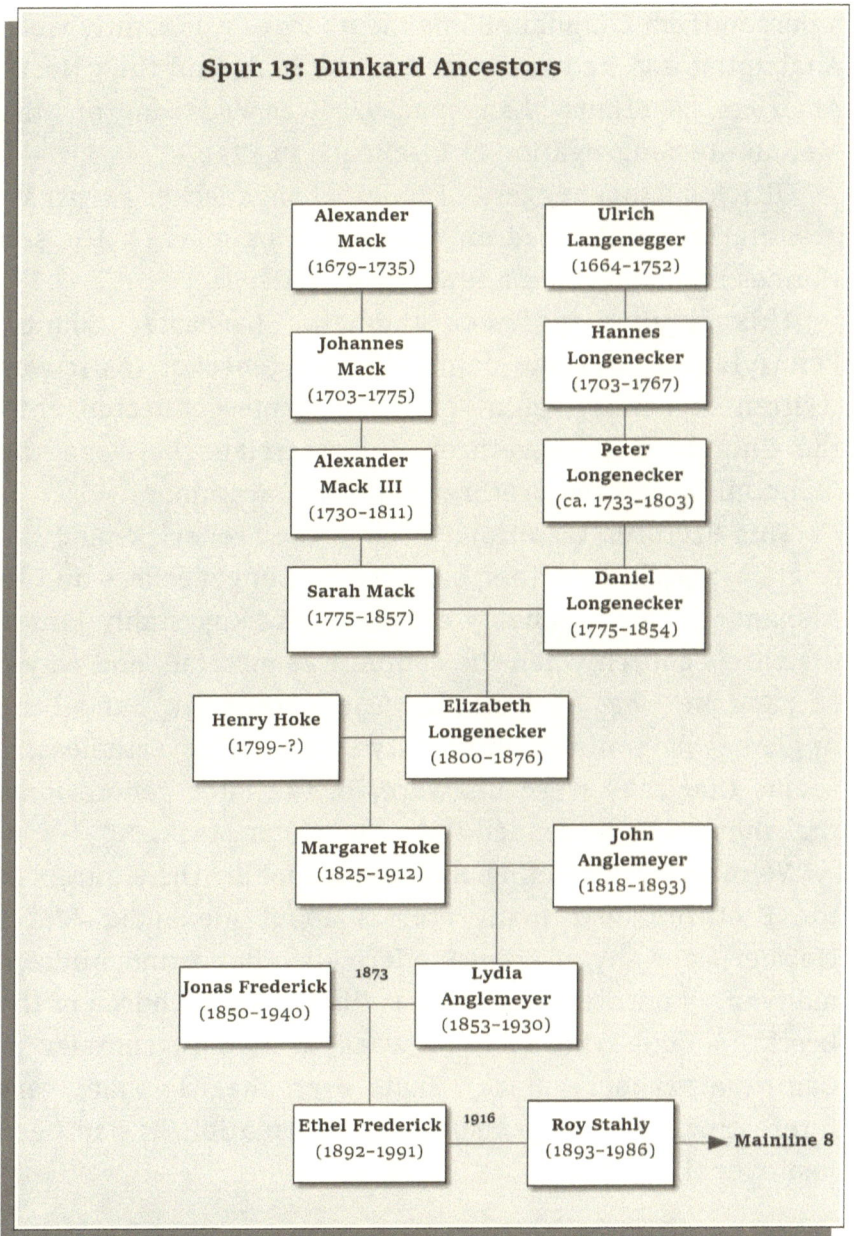

Spur 13: Dunkard Ancestors

Alexander Mack (1679–1735)
Johannes Mack (1703–1775)
Alexander Mack III (1730–1811)
Sarah Mack (1775–1857)

Ulrich Langenegger (1664–1752)
Hannes Longenecker (1703–1767)
Peter Longenecker (ca. 1733–1803)
Daniel Longenecker (1775–1854)

Henry Hoke (1799–?)
Elizabeth Longenecker (1800–1876)

Margaret Hoke (1825–1912)
John Anglemeyer (1818–1893)

Jonas Frederick (1850–1940) — 1873 — Lydia Anglemeyer (1853–1930)

Ethel Frederick (1892–1991) — 1916 — Roy Stahly (1893–1986) ► Mainline 8

The **Longenecker** family was of Swiss origin, from the area around Langnau in the Emmental. The original Swiss spelling of the name was/is "Langenegger," which denotes a person from Langnau. Some members of this family were Anabaptist and had emigrated to the Pfalz and then North America. A Hans Langenacker was deacon of the Mennonite congregation at Fischbach in 1732.

Ulrich Langenegger, Daniel Longenecker's great-grandfather, emigrated on the ship *Hope* in 1733. His son Hannes had emigrated a few years earlier.

This family lived near Manheim, Lancaster County, Pennsylvania. At some point, this Longenecker (as it was written in Pennsylvania) branch became connected with the Church of the Brethren—intermarriage between the Mennonites and the Brethren was not uncommon.

This Brethren tradition, through the Fredericks and the Anglemeyers and further back to the Longeneckers and to Alexander Mack, probably explains why Roy Stahly joined his wife's church when the couple was married, and why a re-baptism was required. The Frederick and the Anglemeyer families were firmly Dunkard. Nevertheless, it seems that they were unaware, in the later generations, that they were descended from Alexander Mack.

Youngsters attending Sunday school in the Church of the Brethren hear many stories about Alexander Mack. Neither I nor any of Ethel Frederick's other grandchildren, many of whom were baptized at the Wawaka Church of the Brethren, and who spent a week or two in summer at Camp Alexander Mack, had ever heard that very interesting piece of genealogical information. It had been lost over the years.

6. The Story of the Story

If John Dillinger had been more of model citizen and had not turned to a life of crime, perhaps this book would never have been written.

This chapter tells the story of the story, i.e., the meta-story, of how this Stahly history was uncovered, although much of the history in this book was not discovered by me.

It started (for me) in 1967 when I was a junior in high school, in Tipton, Indiana. As part of an American history course, the teacher assigned a term paper on a topic of Indiana history. For some unremembered reason, I selected Dillinger, and visited the library to check out a biography of the infamous Depression-era gangster.

The story of Dillinger's last robbery, in South Bend in 1934, as I have already related on page 104, was what attracted my attention. I was fascinated by the Stahly connection and inquired of my grandfather, Roy Stahly, whether he knew about the Perry Stahly who was mentioned in the Dillinger book. He did not, but directed me to my third cousin, John I. Stahly, of Nappanee, who was the family historian.

John Stahly had been collecting and documenting family details from at least the early 1960s. He mailed out questionnaires and then documented the information on huge scrolls, which he brought to family reunions and unrolled for everyone to see.

In developing a family tree it is usually necessary, of course, to work backwards. A researcher starts with a known set of individuals and researches their parents, grandparents, etc. Using this approach, John Stahly had created a family tree that reached back to the elder Heinrich Stähli, who was born in 1751 in Germany.

As John and I were third cousins in a large family, we had never met. Our family reunions had never overlapped —we were too distantly related to attend the same family reunion, which most often did not extend beyond first or second cousins. Although I had never met John Stahly, he nonetheless enthusiastically answered my inquiry, and explained how Perry Stahly, the man involved in the South Bend robbery, was related to us. And, more importantly, John effectively sowed the seed of genealogical curiosity.

In that summer of 1967, John Stahly had planned to go to Europe, for a general tour of the continent, and to further explore family history. He invited me to go along. That trip was the first of many for me across the ocean.

While in Germany, we met Staehly relatives in Frankfurt/Main, and at Hof Offenthal near St. Goarshausen. These relatives were people who descended from Jacob Stähli (1752–1822), and his wife Elisabeth Brennemann.

We also visited Heidelberg, where I would later spend part of my college life. This beautiful city was one of the principal seats of government for the Pfalz, where the Stählis had lived for over 100 years. At the time, I was unaware that a well-known ancestor of mine, Alexander Mack, had been born across the Neckar, in Schriesheim, in 1679.

For many years, the research of John Stahly was "stuck" at the 1750 generation. He knew that the elder Heinrich Stähli (1751–1826) had been born in Germany, and that his son, also Heinrich, had emigrated to the United States in 1835. Of course, he also knew that "Stähli" was a Swiss surname, but had found no evidence about where, exactly, in Switzerland, the family had originated. Without a place of origin, research in the Swiss records was impossible, since it was unknown which parish should be searched.

One theory was that this Indiana Stähli family came from Oberhofen am Thunersee. Another Stähli family, originally from Oberhofen, had emigrated to Illinois in the 1850s. This family was Amish-Mennonite and spelled their surname "Stahly"—exactly as the earlier-arriving Indiana Stahly family. It seemed a reasonable assumption that the two families were somehow connected. But no connection had ever been found.

In 2001, John Stahly made another trip to Germany, searching for clues, and this time he found what he was looking for, at the Weierhof Mennonite research library. A newly published book—*Bürgerbuch der Verbandsgemeinde Hochspeyer, 1650-1850,*[1] by Franz Neumer—provided information that connected the elder Heinrich Stähli (born 1751) with his father and grandfather, and mentioned Sigriswil.

This was the first clue that the family originated in Sigriswil. With that discovery, research moved several generations backward in time, and further research could be undertaken using the Swiss archives.

Heidelberg, from the Philosophenweg (Philosopher's Way)

---

1   The title, in English, is: "Citizen Book of the Municipality of Hochspeyer." The municipality of Hochspeyer consisted of that village, and several others in the neighborhood. The book is not available in English.

By the time of his discovery of this crucial book, in Germany, John Stahly and I had been out of touch for many years, although he had continued his research. His scrolls and other paper files had been entered into a computerized database, and John published a booklet summarizing the Stahly history as it was known at the time.

After John Stahly and I reconnected, he asked for my help in researching the Swiss records, reasoning that my German language skills, learned in college, would be needed in reading the old parish registers.

The Swiss in Canton Bern have been diligent in maintaining these parish registers. The records had been microfilmed by the Mormons, and, at that time, could only be viewed, on request, in Family History Centers in North America. John and I had our first look at the Sigriswil parish registers in the Family History Center in Mishawaka, Indiana, in 2002.

We started with a death entry in the Neumer book, which indicated that a Caspar Stähli (presumed grandfather of Heinrich Stähli, born 1751), from Sigriswil, had died in 1732 in the Pfalz, at age 40, and with a calculated birth year of about 1692. The first task was to see whether this Caspar's baptismal record could be found in the Sigriswil parish records.

At first glance, it seemed impossible that these records could ever be comprehensible. The microfilm readers at the Family History Center were awkward, and the ancient handwriting of the records was very small and indecipherable—at least at first glance.

The initial experience looking at the Sigriswil parish register was therefore slightly discouraging. Nothing definitive was found. I did make copies of the relevant pages from the church book, and with patience and practice, at home, it eventually became possible for me to read the handwriting.

A posting of an extract (that I thought looked promising) to an online forum brought a helpful response from Swiss genealogist Peter Wälti. He answered that the extract in question did, in fact, refer to the Stähli family, and that a 1691 baptismal record of Peter indicated that the family was from Aeschlen (near Sigriswil), and that the father, Caspar Stähli, had died at some point before the baptism of his son.

This was not what I was hoping for. I wanted a Caspar Stähli born in 1691/92, and what I had was a Peter Stähli, whose father, Caspar, had already died by that time.

Long-time family researchers will be familiar with this situation. Whenever a discovery confounds expectations, denial ensues. In this case, my reaction was that perhaps Peter Stähli's middle name was Caspar, which he then started using later in life. Or, maybe the person who recorded the baptism made an error in writing down the name. All kinds of implausible scenarios spring to mind to account for the fact that the data conflicts with expectations. Fortunately, this denial stage only lasts a few days—usually.

After I had reserved the microfilm of the Sigriswil parish registers at a Family History Center close to home, I began to reconstruct the details of this Stähli family. The fact that the records from before 1671 had been lost in a fire was unfortunate, but I was able to create a picture of the family, from 1673 through 1691.

As shown in Chapter 1, there were two sons named Caspar born to this family, one of whom had died by 1685, when the second Caspar was baptized.

This baptismal record of the second son named Caspar had its own issues with regard to its ambiguous language, but the fundamental question at first was whether this child became the man referenced in the 1732 death notice, as recorded in the Neumer book.

The inconsistency between the German death record and the contents of the Sigriswil baptismal record was perplexing, and occupied John and me for many months. Eventually, I noticed that Neumer, when he transcribed the original death entry from the Waldfischbach parish register, to include in his book, had, when specifying the dead man's age as 40, appended a question mark. This (presumably) meant that there was some uncertainty, somewhere. Neumer had also used a question mark when specifying the calculated birth year, 1692.

This situation, which I have described more fully on page 60, provides an excellent example of why it is always preferable to research primary sources, if it is at all possible. In this case, the primary source for the death record, the Waldfischbach parish register, was ambiguous about Caspar's age at the time of his death. This ambiguity was the reason for the question marks in Neumer's transcription. One reading of the death entry was that Caspar Stähli was 40 years old when he died. But it was also plausible, from the handwriting, that he was 47 years old at his death in 1732, which would make the 1685 baptism a perfect fit.

Of course, that perfect fit was meaningless if the child born in 1685 had died at or shortly after his birth, as the language in the baptismal record seemed to suggest. This issue took several more years to resolve. The majority of the native German speakers to whom I showed the entry thought that the child, Caspar, had died. A few disagreed; some only said that it wasn't clear. Since no other entries related to Caspar Stähli could be found in the Sigriswil parish register, some other evidence was required.

In 2003, a few years after I had discovered the 1685 baptismal record, John and I decided we needed the services of a professional genealogist in Switzerland, someone who could research archives that were not generally available in the United States.

Therese Metzger was chosen for this project. After I sent her the relevant material (background, copies of the baptismal records, etc.), she declined to undertake the research. She felt that it was clear from the baptismal record that the child Caspar had died, and that it would be a waste of time and money to pursue it any further. This, of course, was extremely discouraging. Fortunately, Metzger wrote back a few days later to say that she had given it more thought, had reviewed the material again, and thought that, although the language in the baptismal record was certainly confusing, it was reasonable to continue research.

And so, Metzger went to the city of Bern, where the cantonal archives (*Staatsarchiv des Kantons Bern*) are located. On her first day there, and within a few hours, she found the key document: a sales contract from 1713 which detailed the transfer of property of Caspar Stähli to his brother-in-law, Jacob Racheter.

Since I knew that Caspar Stähli's elder sister, Anna, had married Jacob Racheter in 1703, this was conclusive evidence that the child born in 1685 had indeed survived, and that, in selling his property and giving up his communal rights, Caspar Stähli was preparing to emigrate.

This sales contract and the baptismal record from 1685 proved to be the crucial pieces of evidence found in the Swiss archives.

Even so, it was difficult to let go of the Oberhofen theory. The two villages, Sigriswil and Oberhofen, are very close, and it seemed probable that the two families were related. However, the Hilterfingen parish register, which had survived over the years entirely intact, contained no indication at all that there was any connection.

Several years later, y-chromosome testing of male descendants from the Sigriswil and Oberhofen clans proved that there was no common male ancestor for the two lines.[2] Still, despite all the contrary evidence, numerous online family trees erroneously connect the two families.

A few other documents found in the cantonal archives offered scant clues about the Stähli family in Sigriswil. Several sales contracts relating to property in Aeschlen described pieces of land that had changed hands, as mentioned in Chapter 1, but it is not clear whether these sales contracts are referring to Caspar Stähli, who married

---

2 DNA testing has shown that the Stähli families from various places in Canton Bern and Canton Zürich are not related along paternal lines. On the other hand, DNA testing did confirm that the Staehly family in Germany was from the same paternal lineage as the Indiana Stahlys. DNA testing confirmed that the child Johannes, later John Johnson, could not have been fathered by his mother's husband, Heinrich Stähli. Y-chromosome testing was also crucial in connecting Ulrich Steely with the Stähli family.

Benedichta Saurer, or to his father. Likewise, baptismal records found in the parish registers referred to a Caspar Stähli of Aeschlen, in 1653 and 1663, but again it is not absolutely clear which one is meant.

The Neumer book contains a list of the children, all born in the Pfalz, of Caspar Stähli and Magdalena Schedeberger. Finding the original sources for this information was challenging because the births and baptisms occurred in different locales, although relatively close to each other: Waldfischbach, Sembach, Trippstadt and Hochspeyer.

The 1732 death record of Caspar Stähli (born 1685) was found in the Waldfischbach parish register. The second marriage of his widow, Magdalena, was found in the parish register of the Catholic church at Horbach. All of these primary sources were investigated in order to find clues about the family. The information was scant, but sufficient to connect the family to Sigriswil.

These discoveries were used to expand John Stahly's database, and moved the earliest research backward to about 1650.

Between the baptism of Hans-Jörg Stähli in 1721, and the marriage of his son Heinrich, in 1797, there is almost no paper trail to be found. Whether this is because the paper documents do not exist or whether they are as yet undiscovered is not known. Information about Hans-Jörg and his wife Anna Kinzinger is derived from the marriage and death records of their children, specifically those of Johannes, Heinrich, Jacob and Magdalena.

During the 18th century, the Mennonites had become more accepted in their adopted land of the Pfalz, although they continued to hold themselves apart from the rest of the population. Persecution of the Mennonites had lessened, and this may have allowed them to discontinue the practice of having their children baptized in one of the established churches, which was sometimes done in order to stay on the right side of the authorities and to maintain rights of residence. Ironically, the improved atmosphere for the Mennonites in the Pfalz may have indirectly caused fewer records to be kept about them.

While they resided at Diemerstein, the Stähli family probably belonged to the Sembach Mennonite (*Mennonitengemeinde* Sembach) congregation.[3] This congregation constructed their first church building in 1777. Prior to that, services were held in private homes. There was also a building at Diemerstein that was used for services by the Mennonites.

Mennonite Church in Sembach (2015)

---

3 Although the baptism of Hans-Jörg Stähli in 1721 was recorded in the Sembach parish register, it was the register of the Reformed congregation.

Baptism of infants, of course, was not a practice of the Mennonites, so the official registration of newborns with the local authorities may not have been done. Perhaps the records have simply remained undiscovered, or have been lost.

This lack of conventional documentation from the middle part of the 18th century can be compensated for, to some extent, by the relatively detailed records that were created by civil authorities starting in about 1800.

After the American and French revolutions, ideas in Europe about the role of a state-sponsored church and religious freedom started slowly to evolve. Although religious freedom was by no means universal, increasingly tolerant attitudes had started to become more prevalent. Civil authorities, rather than ecclesiastical ones, began to maintain the official records for births, marriages and deaths.

Starting with the marriage of Heinrich Stähli, the elder, in 1802, birth, marriage, and death records were recorded by civil authorities, either by the French while the family was at St. Germanshof, or by the German civil authorities, under the king of Bavaria, after the family had returned to Diemerstein, and the French had given up their rule of the Pfalz.

*

After John Stahly died in 2007, I became the *de facto* custodian of his database, which contains thousands of names and stretches from about 1650 well into the 20th century. My main contribution to this database has been, for the most part, the data from the Swiss research.

*

Some have wondered whether the Stähli research could be extended further into the past than where it now stands (i.e., about 1650). Unfortunately, the loss of the Sigriswil parish records from before 1671 makes it extremely difficult to locate and verify data from before that. Any earlier details would come from other kinds of records, which certainly could exist, but which so far have not been found.

One clue appears in the book, *600 Jahre Sigriswil 1347–1947*, published in 1947 in recognition of the 600th anniversary of Sigriswil's independence. In that book, the author, Adolf Schaer-Ris, lists town and community officials for Sigriswil from the early 1600s.

Hans Stähli is designated as the *Statthalter, 1628–1637*. The person holding this office served as a representative of the regional or cantonal government. As this was not typically a position for a younger man, it can be assumed that Hans Stähli, *Statthalter*, was (perhaps) between 40 and 50 years old at the time he held office.

If Caspar Stähli, the elder, who had died by 1673, was between 50 and 60 years old at the time of his death, he could have been the son of Hans Stähli, *Statthalter*, and therefore was born between 1610-1620. The line of descent would be as shown in the speculative chart on page 174.

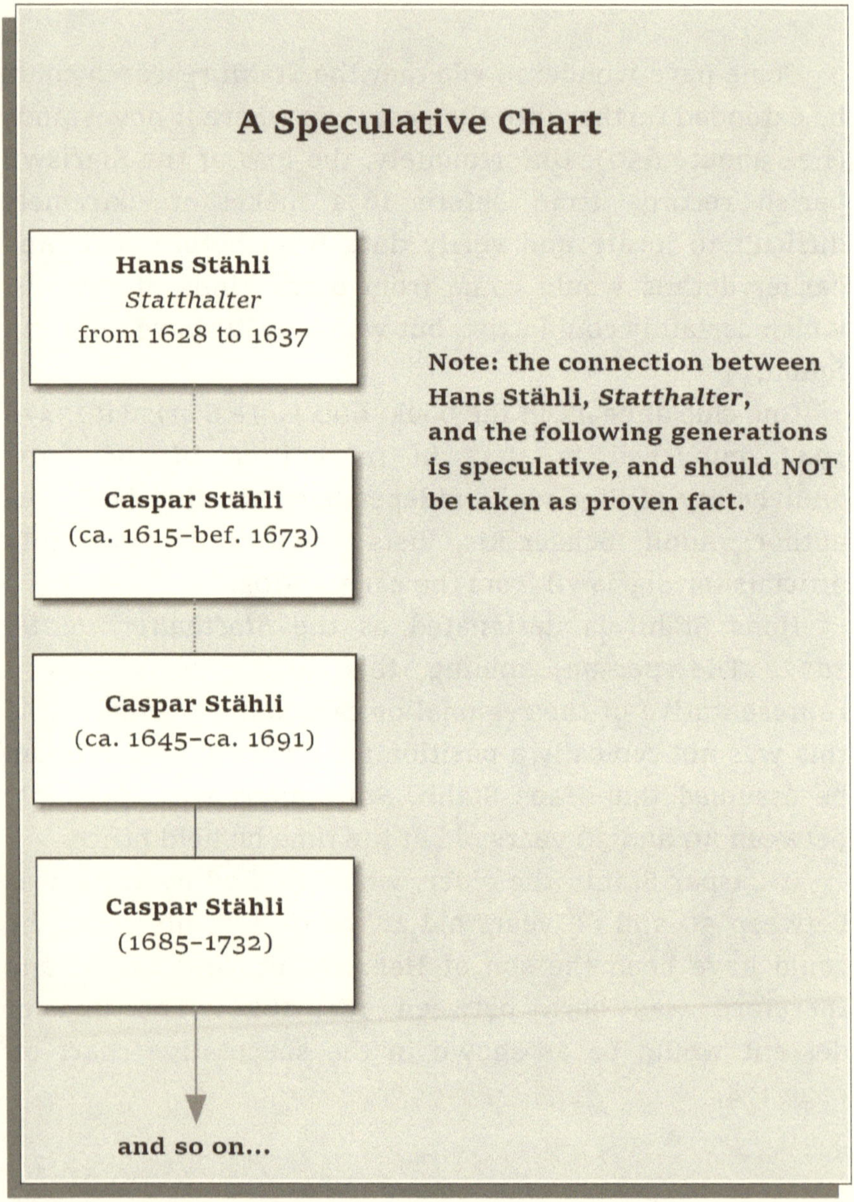

A Speculative Chart

Hans Stähli
Statthalter
from 1628 to 1637

Note: the connection between
Hans Stähli, *Statthalter*,
and the following generations
is speculative, and should NOT
be taken as proven fact.

Caspar Stähli
(ca. 1615–bef. 1673)

Caspar Stähli
(ca. 1645–ca. 1691)

Caspar Stähli
(1685–1732)

and so on...

Of course, this is speculation. It should not be taken as fact. Although the dates fit together nicely, there is <u>no</u> substantive proof for the line of descent shown on the chart. Hans Stähli, the *Statthalter*, could just have easily been on a collateral line—an uncle or cousin, for example. I have not incorporated this information into my database.

I have continued to add to the database, concentrating on collateral or maternal lines. Specifically, I have researched the Künzi (Kinzinger), Ehresmann, Smucker, Frederick and Anglemeyer families, all of whom were marriage partners of one of the principal persons in this history. For some of these families, this was fairly easy to accomplish, since much of the work had already been undertaken by others. It was a matter of making the correct connections and verifying the information as much as possible.

Births, marriages and deaths down through current generations are impossible to keep updated, since the Stahly diaspora has spread throughout Germany and the United States.

*

It is rare that an exciting new genealogical discovery appears unexpectedly in my email inbox. That is what happened in February 2023, when I received an email from Family Tree DNA (FTDNA) notifying me that I had a new y-chromosome match.

FTDNA estimates that, on average, there is a 95% probability that the matching participant (Jeff Steely) and

I share a common paternal ancestor who was born circa 1700. This estimate is based solely on the DNA evidence.

Between Jeff's research and my own, we were able to quickly determine that Jeff's ancestor, Ulrich Steely (born 1726, and baptized as "Johannes Ulrich Stähli"), was the younger brother of my own ancestor, Hans Jörg Stähli (born 1721), as discussed on page 64. Thus, our most recent common paternal ancestor is Caspar Stähli, born in 1685.

What was puzzling to me is that I had frequently looked at the 1742 passenger list for the *Francis and Elizabeth*, and although I had noted "Uhllerich Ställy" among the group of Amish-Mennonite men on board, it never occurred to me to investigate him further. I was focused on two other individuals on the list who were my direct ancestors. My assumption had always been that no one from the Stähli family had emigrated in the 18th century. It is a good lesson for me: stay curious, and don't be shy about challenging long-held assumptions.

This is also an excellent example of the value of DNA testing for genealogical purposes. Specifically, y-chromosome testing can be very useful in sorting out paternal lines that may or may not be connected, when other conventional methods of research have been exhausted.

*

The idea of this book had been germinating for a long time. After John Stahly died, it became clear that if the book was going to be written, it would have to be done by me. Given the large number of descendants of the emigrant generation (the four brothers and their sister), this seemed an overwhelming task.

A family history consists of much more than names and dates. To be interesting, it should attempt to sketch the lives of the individuals, as far as they are known, can be discovered, or can be surmised. It is one thing to do this for your own line, where the stories have been (hopefully) passed down. But it is very difficult to do for other lines. For one thing, I am too far removed from those other lines' stories, and for another, there are simply too many of them to include in a single volume that people would actually want to read. Once I realized that the key to getting this history on paper was to narrow its scope, the book began to take shape.

Nevertheless, this is not the end of the story. The next section offers some suggestions on how interested and motivated readers may use the material in this book to extend and expand the story.

Afterword

Family members reading this book will not find their name in the index. By design, no living person is included in this family history. The latest birth year of any family member explicitly named in this book is 1938.

Of course, readers of this book will likely know exactly where he or she fits in. My hope is that this book will provide the basis for readers and/or descendants to undertake their own research, and to document it, using the data here as a starting point.

This applies not only to descendants of Roy Stahly and Ethel Frederick, but also to descendants of any of the collateral branches discussed here, and for which no great detail is included in this book.

Starting with the 1750 generation, i.e., the children of Hans-Jörg Stähli and Anna Kinzinger, there are many siblings whose heritage is not on the "mainline" of this family history. These may be "branches" in the context of this book, but they are on the "mainline" for many people, and should be researched.

Siblings of marriage partners also provide a rich subject for research. In particular, Sarah Smucker (1859-1916), and Ethel Frederick (1892-1991) each had many siblings, and there are numerous cousins who descend from these lines. These cousins are no less important or interesting than cousins from the "mainline," and it would be worthwhile for motivated researchers to investigate their stories.

To encourage people to document their own history and to update the stories in this book with their own families' data, I will provide a database as a starting point. This file uses a standard genealogical data communications (i.e., gedcom file) format, and can be imported into any commercially available program for amateur genealogists.

For further details about this, contact me at the email address in the author profile at the end of this book.

Acknowledgments

Grateful thanks and acknowledgment are due to the following individuals, each of whom has, in his or her own way, made this book possible.

Much of the genealogical information in this book is based on data collected and compiled by John I. Stahly (1938-2007). He collected and compiled thousands of names and dates. Only a fraction of them appear here, but this book would not have been possible without his invaluable contribution.

Mary Lou Troyer transcribed John Stahly's paper files into a computerized database, into which all of my subsequent research has been incorporated. Mary Lou was also a life-saver by providing a backup copy of the database after I lost my own files in a house fire in 2009.

In Switzerland, Marianne Amstutz-Vogt has been of great help with issues relating to *Gemeinde* Sigriswil. Her hospitality, assistance and insights during my visits have enriched this story in many ways.

Helmut Gingerich in Bavaria has been very helpful in finding documents in the German archives, and helping me to decipher and understand them. Whenever I come across a fragment of indecipherable handwriting in an old document, I know I can count on him. His thorough and exacting skills have contributed many details to my own research.

Herbert Holly, a Stähli descendant as well as a chronicler of the Mennonites in Bavaria, alerted me to the existence of an entire branch of the family in the United States of which I had not been aware.

Helmut Suttor in Frankfurt/Main has extensively researched the Suttor family, and in doing so has provided many helpful details about the Stähli family, from whom he also descends.

Swiss professional genealogists Therese Metzger and Peter Wälti have worked diligently in the Bernese cantonal archives to locate and transcribe crucial records pertaining to the Stähli family in Switzerland.

Jean Fitts Cochrane read the initial draft of this book. Her insights, suggestions and advice are very much appreciated.

My cousin Maggie Rost (née Loveless) gave me the nudge that I needed to get this book underway.

Cousins and other family members have contributed their memories, photographs and stories, without which this history would have remained a list of names and dates.

My late parents, Daniel Stahly and Mabel Wright, were always interested in my hobby, and encouraged me along the way. The fact that they allowed their 17 year old son to travel to Europe in 1967 with a distant cousin speaks for itself.

Tom van Cleve, my partner of many years, has likewise always provided support and encouragement. Like my father and grandfather, I married "outside the clan"—in more ways than one. Fortunately, Tom is also interested in family history, and has been very supportive of my obsession, as well as being reasonably tolerant of my so-called Mennonite-like taste in clothing.

*

One feature of genealogical research is that errors persist, despite one's best efforts. Although many people have contributed to this project, I accept responsibility for the errors that doubtless exist in this book.

Bibliography

Books

Ford, Ira, *et alia*, *The History of Northeast Indiana*, (Chicago and New York, Lewis Publishing, 1920).

Guth, Hermann, *Amish Mennonites in Germany*, (Morgantown, PA, Masthof Press, 1995).

Guth, Hermann and Gertrude; Mast, J. Lemar and Lois Ann, *Palatine Mennonite Census Lists, 1664–1793*, (Morgantown, PA, Masthof Press, 1987).

Hecht, Dirk, *Geschichte der Stadt Schriesheim*, (Ubstadt-Weiher, Verlag Regionalkultur, 2014).

Holt, Steven M., *A History of the Amish*, (Intercourse, PA, Good Books, 2003).

Hostetler, Harvey, *Descendants of Jacob Hochstetler, the immigrant of 1736*, (Elgin, IL, Brethren Publishing, 1912).

Hostetler, Harvey, *Descendants of Barbara Hochstedler and Christian Stutzman*, (Berlin, OH, Gospel Book Store, 1938).

Hostetler, Paul V., *The Three Zug (Zook) Brothers of 1742 and their Male Descendants until 1850*, (Morgantown, PA, Masthof Press, 1982).

Miller, J. Virgil, *Anniversary History of the Family of John "Hannes" Miller, Sr.*, (Morgantown, PA, Masthof Press, 1998).

Müller, Ernst, *History of the Bernese Anabaptists*, (Aylmer, ON, Pathway Publishers, translation 2010 by John A. Gingerich).

Neumer, Franz, *Bürgerbuch der Verbandsgemeinde Hochspeyer*, 1650–1850, (Otterbach, Verlag Franz Arbogast, 1995).

Ruby, Arnold, *Verbandsgemeinde Enkenbach-Alsenborn, Ihre Bürger 1650–1850*, (Ludwigshafen am Rhein, Verlag der Arbeitsgemeinschaft Pfälzisch-Rheinische Familienkunde e.V., 1982).

Schaer-Ris, Adolf, *Sigriswil*, (Bern, Verlag Paul Haupt, 1979).

Schaer-Ris, Adolf, *600 Jahre Sigriswil 1347-1947*, (Sigriswil, Kommissionsverlag des Einwohnergemeinderates, 1947).

Schrock, Elden R., *The Family of Barbara and John Ringenberg*, (Nappanee, IN, Elden R. Schrock, 1979).

Smucker, Silas J., *Christian Schmucker*, (Goshen, IN, Silas J. Smucker, 1986).

Smucker, Silas, J, and **Esther V.**, *Ancestors and Descendants of Jonathan P. Smucker,* (Milford, IN, Kosko Printers, 1976).

Springer, Joe A., *Montbéliard Mennonite Church Register, 1750-1958*, (Goshen, IN, Mennonite Historical Society, 2015).

Stoltzfus, Nic, *German Lutherans to Pennsylvania Amish: the Stoltzfus Family Story,* (Morgantown, PA, Masthof Press, 2019).

Strassburger, Ralph Beaver, *Pennsylvania German Pioneers,* (Norristown, PA, Pennsylvania German Society, 1934).

Yoder, Paton, and **Smucker, Silas J.,** *Jonathan P. Smucker,* (Goshen, IN, Silas J. Smucker, 1990).

Journals

"Chorgericht und Landvogt in Behandlung der Täufergeschäfte," *Blätter für bernische Geschichte, Kunst und Altertumskunde,* volume 24, 1928.

"The Strange Case of Hans Zaugg," Darvin L. Martin, *Mennonite Family History,* January 2023.

"From Steffisburg to Ste. Marie-aux-Mines: the Exodus of those who would become Amish," Robert Baecher, *Mennonite Family History,* January and April 2004.

"Locke, Indiana: the Making of a Ghost Village," James Lamar Weyland, *Indiana Magazine of History,* March 1977.

Herald of Truth and *Gospel Herald,* Mennonite weekly magazines, published obituaries of many Amish-Mennonite persons, available at: http://www.mcusa-archives.org/MennObits

Archives

Staatsarchiv des Kantons Bern: Bernese parish registers, and legal files from the district of Thun.
Parish registers are also available online at:
http://www.query.sta.be.ch/

Kirchenportal GmbH has archived most German parish registers, available at:
https://archion.de

Archives Départementales du Bas-Rhin: Civil birth, marriage and death records, available at:
https://archives.bas-rhin.fr/

National Archives of the United States: Passenger lists of vessels arriving at New York, and United States Census records, 1840-1940. Many of these records are also available at https://www.ancestry.com

Pennsylvania State Archives

Kansas State Archives

Fort Wayne News-Sentinel Archives at:
https://news-sentinel.newsbank.com/

Nappanee Advance-News Archives at:
https://newspapers.library.in.gov/

Online Resources

Ancestry: https://www.ancestry.com
Find-a-Grave: https://www.findagrave.com
GAMEO, Anabaptist Encyclopedia: http://www.gameo.org
Geneal Forum: https://geneal-forum.com/
LDS Family Search: https://www.familysearch.org/
Schweizerischer Verein für Täufergeschichte:
    http://mennonitica.ch
Swiss Anabaptist Genealogical Association:
    http://www.saga-omii.org

Other Resources

First Mennonite Church, 75th Anniversary, 1875–1950,
    (Nappanee, IN, First Mennonite Church, 1950).

Schmidt, Hans Jörg, *"Religion made in Schriesheim.*
    Der Kirchenbegründer Alexander Mack,"
    transcript of a lecture.

Staker, Joseph Peter, *Amish Mennonites in Tazewell*
    County, Illinois, (online only).

.
Steely Family Tree, compiled by Jeff Steely.

Yoder Family Newsletter:
    http://yoderfamilynewsletter.org

Illustrations

Photographs, unless otherwise credited, are either by the author or are family photographs in the author's possession.

The artwork by Jakob Samuel Weibel is in the public domain, from the Swiss National Library.

On the back cover, the drawing of a farm in Locke Township, Elkhart County, is from *An Illustrated Historical Atlas of Elkhart Co., Indiana*, published in 1874 by Higgins Belden & Co.

The extract from a plat map on page 113 is from *Standard Atlas of Elkhart County, Indiana*, published in 1915 by Geo. A. Ogle & Co.

The family charts are the creation of the author.

Index

Author Profile

Bruce W. Stahly was born at Wolf Lake, Indiana, a few miles from the Eagle Lake farm where his father grew up. He attended school at Wawaka, Cromwell and Tipton, and spent his college years at Hanover College and the University of Heidelberg. After a career in computers and software, Bruce and his partner moved to northern Minnesota, where he worked in his ideal job at an independent bookstore. Now retired, he continues his life-long interest in family history. He hopes that other family members will use the information in this book to document their own stories. He can be reached at **bws0813@gmail.com**.